Time-Crunch Quilts

NANCY J. MARTIN

Martingale
& COMPANY

Bothell, Washington

CREDITS

President . . . . Nancy J. Martin
CEO/Publisher . . . . Daniel J. Martin
Associate Publisher . . . . Jane Hamada
Editorial Director . . . . Mary V. Green
Design and Production Manager . . . . Cheryl Stevenson
Technical Editor . . . . Ursula Reikes
Copy Editor . . . . Ellen Balstad
Illustrator . . . . Laurel Strand
Photographer . . . . Brent Kane
Cover and Text Designer . . . . Rohani Design

That Patchwork Place is an imprint of Martingale & Company.

MISSION STATEMENT

We are dedicated to providing quality products and service by working together to inspire creativity and to enrich the lives we touch.

Time-Crunch Quilts
© 2000 by Nancy J. Martin

Martingale & Company
PO Box 118
Bothell, WA 98041-0118 USA
www.patchwork.com

Printed in China
05 04 03 02 01 00   6 5 4 3 2 1

ACKNOWLEDGMENTS

I would like to thank the following people:

Alvina Nelson, whose lovely quilting stitches graced the "Lady of the Lake" wedding quilt made for Mike and Terry Martin;

Cleo Nollette, for providing "Christmas Nine Patch," "Ann's Little Nine Patch," "Cake Stand," "Delectable Mountains," "Woodland Spring," and "Quilts in the Attic";

Amanda Miller's fine quilters: Mary Hershberger, Bena Miller, Elsie Raber, Irene Schwartz, Bertha Stutzman, Clara Stutzman, Clara Troyer, Martha Troyer, Sarah Troyer, Fannie Yoder, and MaryAnn Yoder;

Pam Klopfer, for computer entry and general helpfulness;

Ursula Reikes, my editor, for her usual thorough job of editing;

Laurel Strand, for her wonderful illustrations. Thank goodness you are a quilter!

Brent Kane, for his great quilt photography; and

all the staff at Martingale & Company for your hard work, dedication, and support. What a team!

Library of Congress Cataloging-in-Publication Data

Martin, Nancy J.
    Time crunch quilts / Nancy J. Martin.
        p. cm.
    ISBN 1-56477-291-8
        1. Patchwork—Patterns. 2. Quilting—Patterns.
    3. Patchwork quilts. I. Title.

TT835 .M27343 2000
746.46—dc21   99-053393

Ann's Little Nine Patch by Cleo Nollette.

To Cleo Nollette

You have helped me in every imaginable time crunch. The deadline may call for stitching quilt tops, baby-sitting for Dad Martin or Megan, cooking a gourmet meal for forty, or shopping for props, and you are always equal to the task. Your precise sewing skills, great sense of humor, wonderful gourmet treats, and expertise with my MasterCard are all so very helpful. Your calling card says Assistant to the President, but I just like to call you my special friend.

Contents

Sawtooth Mountains by Nancy J. Martin

Introduction

What would you say if I told you it is possible to stitch twenty quilts in one year? Would you say it's impossible? Then what would you say if I told you that I stitched more than twenty quilts over the past year, and at least six of them were queen size or larger? Knowing that time would be a limiting factor, I carefully planned the quilts so that they would be quick to piece. Four of these quilts needed to be quite special, since they were to be presented to employees who were celebrating their tenth year of employment at That Patchwork Place/Martingale & Company. When I reflected on the making of all these quilts, I realized that I had formulated quite a few tips and shortcuts that would be helpful to other quilters, and therein lies the secret for *Time-Crunch Quilts*.

Each of the twenty quilts illustrates one or more time-crunch features. The quilts vary in size and theme, and several reflect popular holidays. I have included a variety of color schemes and fabric selections.

While many shortcuts are employed in *Time-Crunch Quilts*, there are certain quiltmaking standards to which one must adhere. Take time to read the "Basic Quiltmaking" and "Finishing" sections so that you know why a quilt is constructed in a certain manner.

Fabrics for Time-Crunch Quilts

For best results, select lightweight, closely woven, 100 percent cotton fabrics. Fabrics with a polyester content may make small patchwork pieces difficult to cut and sew accurately.

Although I enjoy making scrap quilts, it is much faster and easier to select only three or four fabrics for your quilt. You will have less fabric to handle and cut, and less color and value decisions to make as you stitch. If using only three fabrics in your quilt, make sure they are interesting fabrics that contrast well. "Delectable Mountains" on page 40 is a good example of a quilt with three contrasting fabrics.

To select fabrics for your quilt, first look to see if your quilt has a background on which a pattern will appear. Most quilts do. If so, select your background first. Don't limit your choices to solid colors, even though muslin is a traditional background fabric. If you really want to use a solid-colored fabric, try a deep turkey red or perhaps black or navy for an Amish look. Remember that solid-colored fabrics tend to emphasize mismatched seams and irregular quilting stitches.

If you are a beginner who is still perfecting your piecing and quilting skills, select a print for your background that will help hide minor imperfections. A background print that is nondirectional and still appears unified after being cut apart and resewn is a good choice. Prints with a white background have a clean, formal look; those with a beige or tan background resemble antique quilts and have a more informal look. Study the examples below for good choices of background fabric.

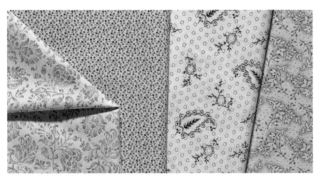

Nondirectional background fabrics

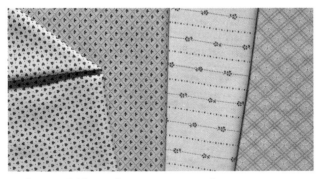

Background fabrics that require special cutting

To test the suitability of background fabrics while shopping, make several directional folds and evaluate the unity of the design, as shown in the illustration below.

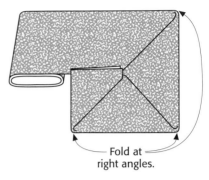

Fold at right angles.

Once you have chosen the background fabric, select the remaining fabrics that will enhance it. Study the colors that appear in the design on the background fabric and begin your selection. If you are working with a single color family, such as blue, select a wide range of blue fabrics. Begin with deep, dark navy blues, adding royal blues, medium blues, and light blues. If most of your blue fabrics are bright, stick to bright blues in all shades. If your blue fabrics are dull or "grayed," select muted shades of blue fabrics.

Try to avoid stripes, directional fabrics, and theme prints that require special cutting. However, if you find these fabrics irresistible, I have included some helpful tips to use when cutting (see page 26).

Time-Crunch Features

The time used in designing a time-crunch quilt will be well spent. All decisions on block design, color placement, setting, and borders are made during the design stage. Constructing the quilt then becomes a quick and easy process that is not bogged down by agonizing decisions. Consider the following time-crunch features as you design.

SMALL QUILTS

They say good things come in small packages, and small quilts are no exception. You can use small quilts as the centerpiece on a table, draped over a chair or sofa back, or as a wall hanging. They also make wonderful gifts. If you choose an easy block that can be strip pieced, such as a Nine Patch, your stitching time is markedly decreased. Another advantage of a small quilt is that it can be finished with button tufting (see page 20). A good example of a quickly pieced small quilt is "Christmas Nine Patch" on page 32.

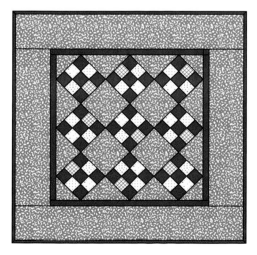

THEME PRINTS

Theme prints refer to fabrics that have a large-scale design that depicts a scene or other large motif. Toile fabrics are among the most popular of the scenic prints. The original toiles, known as Toile de Jouy, date back to 1760 and were printed with copper plates in Jouy, France. There are many toile reproductions available today.

Some fabric manufacturers are now producing large-scale prints that feature many different themes, including coffee, cowboys, paper dolls, botanical prints, and wildlife.

Since these designs are generally quite large, the fabrics are best used in large pieces so that you can see the whole design. If you cut the fabrics into small pieces, you lose the theme. One easy way to use a theme print is to frame it with coordinating fabric in a block like Courthouse Steps or Attic Windows. The blocks are simple to stitch and enhance, rather than compete with, the theme print. See "Woodland Spring" (page 91) and "Quilts in the Attic" (page 99) to see how I used a theme print to make two delightful small quilts.

Courthouse Steps

Attic Windows

"Quilt Talk" (page 95) features a fabric with humorous sayings about quilting. Because the fabric design is based on words rather than pictures, I used a more intricate block to frame the design. If this idea intrigues you but you can't find a fabric with printed sayings, create your own. Write your sayings on fabric, or print them on your computer and transfer them to fabric using a photo-transfer method. A few of my favorite sayings are listed below.

- A quilt is a blanket of love.
- I never met a quilt I didn't like.
- So many fabrics, so little time.
- As ye stitch, so shall ye rip.

LARGE BLOCKS

An easy strategy for making a large quilt quickly is to use large blocks. For example, by setting a 12" Four Corners block on the diagonal and adding four corner triangles, you have a 17" block, which I renamed Corner Star.

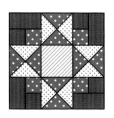

12" block

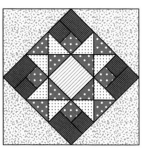

17" block

Another way to create large blocks is to enlarge the size of the units in the block. I usually cut and piece 2½" bias squares, which finish

to 2". In "Lady of the Lake" (page 61), I cut 3" bias squares, which made the finished block 12½" rather than 10". With the addition of sashing strips between the blocks and a wide border, I could construct a queen-size quilt by stitching sixteen Lady of the Lake blocks, rather than twenty-five. By eliminating nine blocks, I needed only 256 bias squares instead of 400! This was a real time saver! I also thought about the setting of the block, which is traditionally set on-point without sashing, as shown below. Although lovely, this setting requires a lot of tedious matching when the blocks are sewn together. Not only does the sashing in my version add additional size to the quilt, but it also saves the time needed to carefully match points.

Lady of the Lake blocks set diagonally

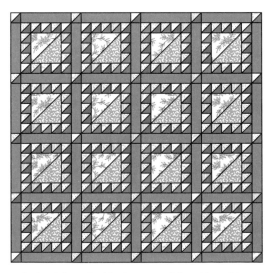

Lady of the Lake blocks set straight with sashing

Framing a small block with strips, as in the Courthouse Steps blocks, also produces large blocks. For example, in "Simple Stars" (page 66), an 8" Star block is enlarged to 14" when it is framed with 1"-wide strips.

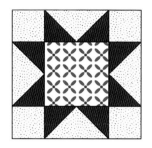
8" Star block

14" Star block

WIDE SASHING

When I first began making quilts, all of the sashing strips used between the blocks finished to either 2" or 2½", regardless of the block size. As I became more experienced in quiltmaking, I discovered that large blocks were nicely balanced by wider sashing. "Doves in the Window" (page 72) was made with 14" blocks and sashing cut 5½" wide. I also found that you can use more interesting large-scale prints when your sashing strips are wide because you see more of the fabric.

Wider sashing also gives you the opportunity to create pieced sashing. While stitching "Wasting Away in Margaritaville" (page 76), I wanted to create movement and add interest to the traditional 12" One Union Square block. The light and dark fabrics in the sashing helped create movement in varying directions. The curved sashing measures 3½" wide after piecing.

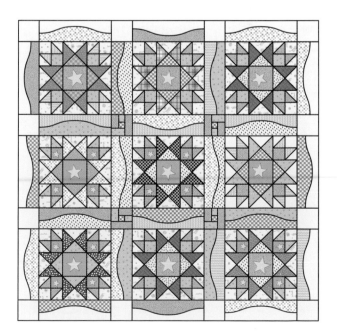

BLOCKS SET DIAGONALLY

Turning a block on-point and setting it with an alternating unpieced block will quickly expand a quilt to a larger size. For example, a 10" block such as Norway Pine (page 48) takes up more than 14⅛" when set diagonally.

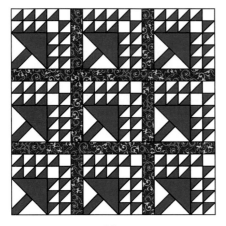

Straight set

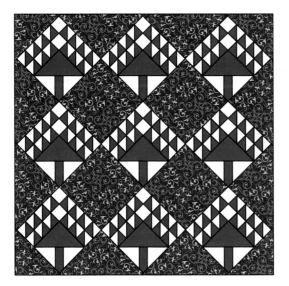

Diagonal set

I like to refer to the alternating blocks as unpieced blocks rather than plain blocks because the fabric you choose is often anything but plain. This is a great opportunity to feature a treasured piece of fabric such as a French Souleiado print, which is best not cut into small pieces. In "Norway Pine," a Souleiado print was also used for the corner and side setting triangles. Souleiado prints, manufactured

in Tarascon, France, are reproductions of old block-printed fabrics.

A 12" One Union Square block will take up almost 17" when set diagonally. To enhance the pieced block, choose an interesting floral print like the one used in "One Union Square" (page 44) for the alternating unpieced block.

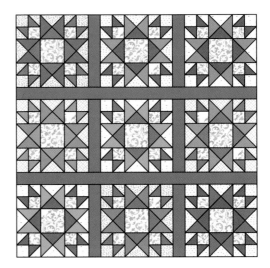

Straight set

Diagonal set

TWO ALTERNATING BLOCKS

Alternating large blocks that are composed of simple units quickly produces a large quilt. In "Nine Patch Stars" (page 81), 13½" blocks containing nine-patch units are alternated with 13½" unpieced blocks with small, machine-appliquéd corner squares. When joined together, the corner squares in the unpieced blocks continue the chain pattern across the quilt, but there is still a large area in the unpieced block for a favorite quilting design.

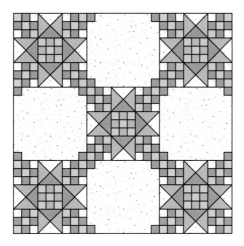

In some cases, the alternating blocks can simply be the alternate placement of the light and dark fabrics. "Woodland Spring" (page 91) uses Courthouse Steps blocks that have light and dark strips in alternating positions.

Using pieced blocks for both of the alternating blocks creates interest and adds movement. "Maple Star Chain" (page 86) uses two blocks—Maple Star and Star Chain. Look for simple blocks such as these that don't require intricate matching when the blocks are joined. Alternating two pieced blocks also creates a secondary pattern across the quilt top.

BIAS-STRIP APPLIQUÉ

I definitely prefer piecing to appliqué. There are times, however, when appliqué is the only answer to a particular design problem. For these situations, I use bias-strip appliqué, a fast and easy solution. For example, the mouths on the pumpkins in "Three Little Pumpkins" (page 107) and the handles in "Tea Party" (page 111) were appliquéd.

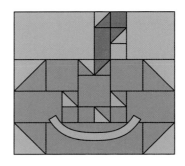

The following steps describe the bias-strip appliqué process.

1. Cut bias strips according to the measurements indicated in the quilt directions.
2. Fold each bias strip in half, wrong sides together, and stitch ⅛" from the edges. Press the tube so that the seam falls in the middle of the back of it.

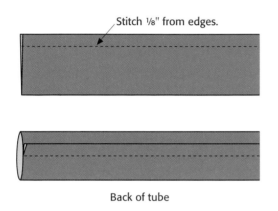

Back of tube

3. Place the bias tube on the background fabric, forming the desired shape. Pin and stitch in place.

BIAS SQUARES

Many traditional quilt patterns contain squares made from two contrasting half-square triangles. The short sides of the triangles are on the straight grain of the fabric while the long sides are on the bias. These are called bias-square units. Using a bias strip-piecing method, you can easily sew and cut bias squares. This technique is especially useful for small bias squares, where pressing after stitching usually distorts the shape (and sometimes burns fingers). The following directions describe an easy way to cut bias squares using 8" squares of fabric.

Note: All directions in this book give the cut size for bias squares; the finished size after stitching will be ½" smaller.

1. Layer two 8" squares of fabric, right sides facing up, and cut in half diagonally.

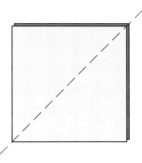

2. Cut into strips, measuring from the previous diagonal cut. Measurements are included in the quilt directions.

3. Arrange and stitch the pieces together, using ¼"-wide seam allowances. Be sure to align the strips so the lower edge and one adjacent edge form straight lines. Press the seams toward the darker fabric.

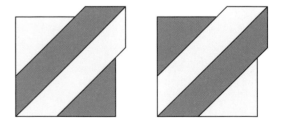

4. Begin cutting at the lower left corner. Align the 45° mark of the Bias Square® ruler on the seam line. Each bias square will require 4 cuts. The first and second cuts are along the side and top edges. They remove the bias square from the rest of the fabric. Make these cuts ¼" larger than the correct size, as shown in the series of illustrations below.

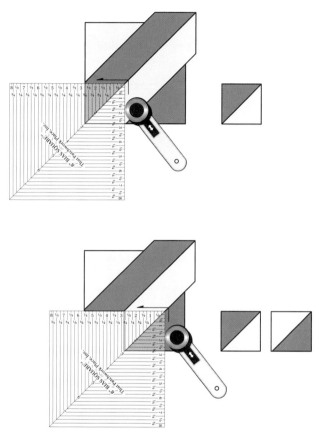

Align 45° mark on seam line and cut first 2 sides.

5. The third and fourth cuts are made along the remaining 2 sides. They align the diagonal and trim the bias square to the correct size. To make the cuts, turn the segment and place the Bias Square ruler on the opposite 2 sides, aligning the required measurements on both sides of the cutting guide and the 45° mark on the seam. Cut the remaining 2 sides of the bias squares.

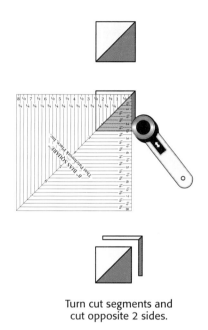

Turn cut segments and cut opposite 2 sides.

6. Continue cutting bias squares from each unit in this manner, working from left to right and from bottom to top, until you have cut bias squares from all usable fabric.

NINE PATCH BLOCKS

Several of the quilts in this book contain Nine Patch blocks and units. Strip piecing is a quick and easy way to mass-produce these blocks. It eliminates the long and tedious repetition of sewing individual pieces together.

To make Nine Patch blocks, first cut strips on the crosswise grain of fabric as shown on pages 24–25. To determine the width to cut the strips, add a ¼"-wide seam allowance to each side of the finished dimension on the desired shape. For example, if the finished dimension of a square will be 2", cut 2½"-wide strips. Strip widths given for all quilts include ¼"-wide seam allowances on each side. Nine Patch blocks are made with two different strip sets.

1. To make Strip Set 1, sew 1 light strip between 2 dark strips, using ¼"-wide seam allowances. Press seams toward the dark fabric.

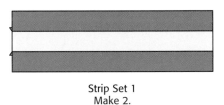

Strip Set 1
Make 2.

2. To make Strip Set 2, sew 1 dark strip between 2 light strips, using ¼"-wide seam allowances. Press seams toward the dark fabric.

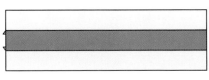

Strip Set 2
Make 1.

3. Place Strip Set 1 and Strip Set 2 together with right sides facing. The seam allowances will face opposite directions.

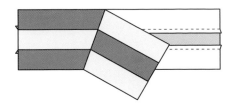

4. Cut the strip sets in pairs. Begin at the left side of the strip and work toward the right. The width of the cut is specified in the directions for each quilt.

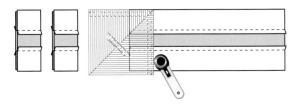

5. Stitch the pairs together with ¼"-wide seam allowances. (See pages 30–31 for chain-piecing directions.)

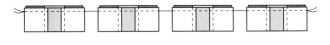

6. Cut the remaining Strip Set 1 into segments the same width as the segments you cut for the pairs.

TIP

If you want strip-pieced units to contain a variety of fabrics instead of identical fabric combinations, vary the strips in the strip sets. Select a different combination of fabrics for each of the strip sets and change the position of the fabrics within the strip sets.

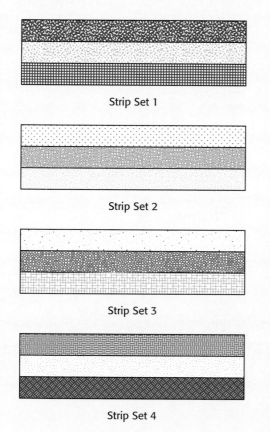

Strip Set 1

Strip Set 2

Strip Set 3

Strip Set 4

For even more scrappy fabric combinations, change the position of the segments within the blocks.

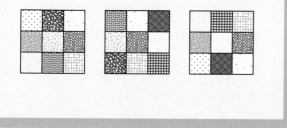

7. Stitch the remaining segments to the previously sewn pairs to complete the Nine Patch blocks.

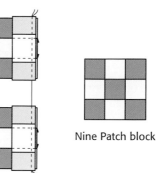

Nine Patch block

8. Press seams as shown.

EASIEST PIECED BORDER IN THE WORLD

The border in "True Blue" (page 56) is an example of the "easiest pieced border in the world." The general rule for this border is that the wider the strips are, the easier the border is to do. This is because there is less piecing to do. The border, however, needs to be proportional to the rest of the quilt. For example, a pieced border of 4"-wide segments might be too big for a small quilt. The "easiest pieced border" works best with quilts made from common-sized blocks such as 6", 8", or 9". The resulting quilt should finish to a measurement that can be divided evenly by a common size such as 2", 3" or 4". For example, if 12" blocks are set four across and four down, the finished quilt measurement will be 48" x 48". Since 48" can be divided evenly by both 3" and 4", the width of the strips in the pieced border can be either 3" or 4" wide.

To make the border, cut strips as indicated in the quilt directions, or the desired finished strip width plus ½" for seam allowances. Join strips to make strip sets and then cut the strip sets into segments the width of the desired border plus ½" for seam allowances. Join the segments as needed to match the measurements of the quilt. The number of strips to cut and the number of segments to cut will depend on the size of your quilt and the desired border width.

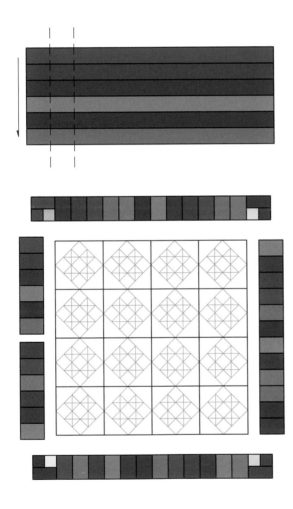

The corner squares in "True Blue" are pieced, but unpieced squares can also be used. Cut squares the same size as the width of the border plus seam allowances.

Here are suggested strip widths to cut for the most common finished block sizes.

Finished Block Size	Strip Width to Cut
6"	2½" or 3½"
8"	2½"
9"	3½"
10"	2½"
12"	3½" or 4½"
14"	2½"
16"	2½" or 4½"

COURTHOUSE STEPS BORDER

Another option for a quick border is to add rows of long strips to opposite sides of a quilt, in the same manner as strips are added to a Courthouse Steps block. An example of this type of border can be seen in "Simple Stars" on page 66. Strips can be as skinny as 1" or as wide as 3" or 4", depending on how large you want the quilt to be. Sew strips to opposite sides and then to the top and bottom edges. Continue adding strips in this manner until you reach the desired quilt size.

EASY QUILTING DESIGNS

Quilting by machine is generally faster than quilting by hand. It is a good choice for those who need to finish their projects in a hurry. It's also a practical and durable choice for items that will be washed many times. However, although machine quilting is faster than hand quilting, selecting the right quilt design can make both types of quilting go a lot faster. Consider the following when choosing a design for quilting:

- A curving or circular design softens the look of angular blocks. Two of my favorites are the Rainbow Fan and Overlapping Circles. The Rainbow Fan is an easy design to quilt because your hand is always moving in a gentle arc, with no awkward angles to manage. Mark the design from the left side if you are left-handed.

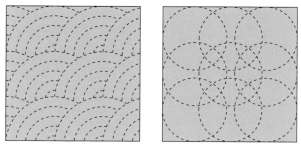

Rainbow Fan   Overlapping Circles

- The tedious process of marking a quilt is avoided if you quilt in the ditch or outline-quilt around pieces (see page 119).
- Masking tape that is ¼"-wide easily marks straight-line designs. Mark one small area at a time and remove the tape as soon as an area is quilted.
- A quilting design that is created with a continuous line saves time. You won't have to stop and bury your knots or drag your quilting thread between the layers.

- Simple straight-line designs quickly fill in space on large, unpieced alternate blocks. See "True Blue" on page 56.

- A continuous, gentle curving design that easily turns a corner is a good choice for quilting borders. My favorite border quilting design was used in "One Union Square on page 44, "Wasting Away in Margaritaville" on page 76, and "Quilt Talk" on page 95.

BUTTON TUFTING

Using buttons is a quick and easy way to secure the layers of a quilt. See "Christmas Nine Patch" on page 32 and "Cake Stand" on page 36 for examples of button tufting. You can use buttons in the same colors as the quilt or use contrasting colors for fun. Shaped buttons, like stars, flowers, or hearts, can also add another dimension to the quilt.

To tack with buttons, lower the feed dogs and set the stitch length at 0. Adjust the stitch width to match the holes in each button. Stitch the buttons, tacking through all three layers.

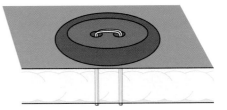

CAUTION

Do not use buttons on quilts for young children since buttons can be pulled off.

Basic Quiltmaking

SUPPLIES

Rotary Cutter and Mat: A large rotary cutter enables you to quickly cut strips and pieces without templates. A cutting mat is essential to protect both the blade and table on which you are cutting. An 18" x 24" mat allows you to cut long strips, on the straight or bias grain. You might also consider purchasing a smaller mat to use when working with scraps.

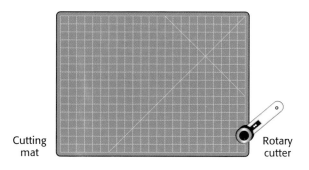

Cutting mat   Rotary cutter

Rotary-Cutting Rulers: Use a long, see-through ruler to measure and guide the rotary cutter. One that is 24" long is a good size. Try to find one that includes markings for 45° and 60° angles, guidelines for cutting strips, and standard measurements. Using a specialized ruler improves cutting accuracy, makes quiltmaking more fun, and frees you from the matching and stitching frustrations that can result from inaccurate cuts.

The Bias Square ruler is critical for cutting accurate bias squares. This acrylic ruler is available in three sizes: 4", 6", or 8" square. It is ruled with ⅛" markings. All sizes feature a diagonal line, which is placed on the bias seam, enabling you to cut two accurately sewn, half-square triangles.

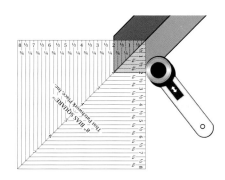

The Bias Square is also convenient to use when cutting small quilt pieces, such as squares, rectangles, and triangles. The larger 8" size is ideal for quick-cutting blocks that require large squares and triangles as well as for making diagonal cuts for half-square and quarter-square triangles.

You can also adapt a general-purpose rotary ruler to work in a similar fashion to the Bias Square.

1. Make a template by cutting a square of see-through plastic in the size specified for the bias square in the quilt directions.
2. Draw a diagonal line on the template, bisecting the square.
3. Tape the template to the corner of an acrylic ruler.

4. Follow the cutting directions given for the quilt you are making, substituting the template-adapted corner of the ruler for the Bias Square.

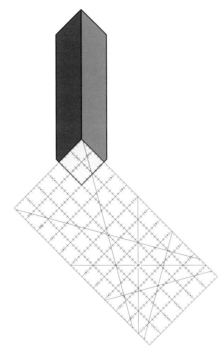

Sewing Machine: Stitching quilts on a sewing machine is easy and enjoyable. Spend some time getting to know your machine and become comfortable with its use. Keep your machine dust-free and well oiled.

Machine piecing does not require an elaborate sewing machine. All you need is a straight-stitch machine in good working order. It should make an evenly locked straight stitch that looks the same on both sides of the seam. Adjust the tension, if necessary, to produce smooth, even seams. A puckered seam causes the fabric to curve, distorting the size and shape of the piecing and the quilt you are making.

Pins: A good supply of glass- or plastic-headed pins is necessary. Long pins are especially helpful when pinning thick layers together.

If you plan to machine quilt, you will need to hold the layers of the quilt together with a large supply of rustproof, size 2 safety pins.

Iron and Ironing Board: Frequent and careful pressing is necessary to ensure a smooth, accurately stitched quilt top. Place your iron and ironing board, along with a plastic spray bottle of water, close to your sewing machine.

Needles: Use sewing-machine needles sized for cotton fabrics (size 70/10 or 80/12). You also need hand-sewing needles (Sharps) and hand-quilting needles (Betweens #8, #9, or #10).

Scissors: Use good-quality shears, and use them only for cutting fabric. Thread snips or embroidery scissors are handy for clipping threads.

Seam Ripper: This little tool will come in handy if you find it necessary to remove a seam before resewing.

YARDAGE REQUIREMENTS

I have often seen the problem created by purchasing too little fabric. There is no flexibility to make the quilt bigger, to make a mistake, or to change your mind. So the fabric requirements given in this book are generous and based on yardage that is 42" wide after prewashing. If your fabric is wider than 42", there will be a little left over at the end of your strips. If your fabric is narrower than 42", you may need to cut an extra strip. Save any extra yardage or strips for future scrap quilts.

Many of the yardage amounts in this book specify fat quarters. This is an 18" x 21" piece of fabric rather than the standard quarter yard that is cut selvage to selvage and measures 9" x 42". The fat quarter is a more convenient size to use, especially when cutting bias strips. Another common size is the fat eighth, which measures 9" x 21". Shops often offer the added convenience of fat quarters and fat eighths already cut and bundled. Look for the basket or bin of fat quarters and fat eighths when selecting fabrics.

FABRIC PREPARATION

Make it a habit to wash and prepare fabrics after you purchase them. Then your fabrics will be ready to sew when you are.

To begin, wash all fabrics first to preshrink, test for colorfastness, and get rid of excess dye. Continue to wash the fabrics until the rinse water is completely clear. Add a square of white fabric to each washing of the fabrics. When this white fabric remains its original color, the fabrics are colorfast. A cupful of vinegar in the rinse water can also be used to help set difficult dyes.

After washing, press the fabrics and fold into fourths lengthwise. Make straight cuts with the rotary cutter across each end. When using the length of fabric, make straight cuts from one end and bias cuts from the other end. Store the fabrics folded.

ROTARY CUTTING

Use and Care of a Rotary Cutter

A rotary cutter has a very sharp blade. It is so sharp that you can cut yourself without even knowing it. If you are not extremely careful, you can also cut other people and objects that you had no intention of slicing. Before you use your rotary cutter for the first time, it is important to know some simple safety rules.

- Close the safety shield when the rotary cutter is not in use.
- Roll the cutter away from yourself. Plan the cutting so your fingers, hands, and arms are never at risk.
- Keep the cutter out of the reach of children.
- Dispose of used blades in a responsible manner. Wrap and tape cardboard around them before placing them in the garbage.

For comfort's sake, think about your posture and the table height as you cut. Stand to cut. You'll find more control than when you sit. Many quilters find they are more comfortable and can work longer if the cutting table is higher than a normal sewing table because they don't have to bend as they cut. If you work on a table that is placed away from a wall, you can easily walk to another side of the table to make your next cut rather than move the fabric or the cutting mat.

If you are left-handed, reverse all cutting directions. Begin by placing the fabric to your left and the ruler to your right. Use a mirror to view the photos. This will help you see the proper cutting alignment.

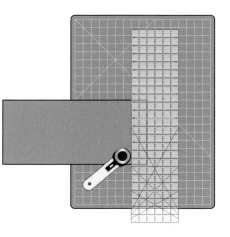

Finally, when the cutting action seems dull with your rotary cutter, try the following suggestion before changing to a new blade. Remove the lint that builds up between the blade and the front sheath of your rotary cutter. Dismantle the cutter, paying close attention to how the pieces go together. Carefully wipe the blade with a soft, clean cloth, adding a small drop of sewing-machine oil to the blade where it lies under the front sheath.

Grain Lines

Fabric is made of threads (called yarns) that are woven together at right angles. This gives fabric the ability to stretch or remain stable, depending on the grain line you use. The lengthwise grain runs parallel to the selvage and has little stretch, while the crosswise grain runs from selvage to selvage and has some give to it. Lines drawn at angles to the straight grain lines are considered bias. A true bias runs at a 45° angle to the lengthwise and crosswise grains and has the most stretch.

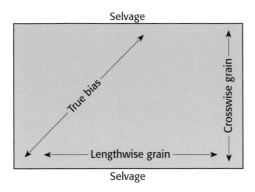

In most cases, the rotary-cutting directions use the following guidelines for grain-line placement:

- All strips are cut on the crosswise grain of the fabric, unless otherwise noted.
- Squares and rectangles are cut on the lengthwise and crosswise grains of fabric.
- Half-square triangles are cut with the short sides on the straight of grain and long side on the bias. The bias square technique produces sewn half-square triangles whose grain lines follow this guideline.
- Quarter-square triangles have the short sides on the bias and the long side on the straight of grain. They are generally used along the outside edges of the quilt, where the long edge will not stretch.
- The straight grain of fabric should fall on the outside edge of all pieced blocks.

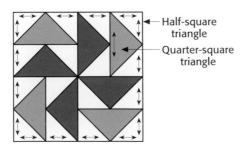

If fabric is badly off-grain, pull diagonally to straighten as shown.

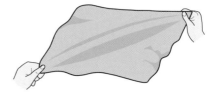

Since many fabrics are printed off-grain, it is impossible to rotary cut fabrics exactly on the straight grain of fabric. In rotary cutting, straight and even cuts are made as close to the grain as possible. A slight variation from the grain will not alter your project.

Cutting Straight Strips

Rotary cutting squares, rectangles, and other shapes begins with cutting strips of fabric. These strips are then crosscut to the proper dimensions. All strip measurements include ¼"-wide seam allowances. Follow these steps to cut strips from the crosswise grain:

1. Fold and press the fabric with selvages matching, aligning the crosswise and lengthwise grains as much as possible. Place the folded fabric on the rotary-cutting mat, with the folded edge closest to your body. Align the Bias Square with the fold of the fabric and place a ruler to the left as shown.

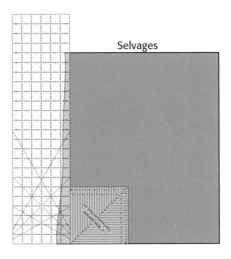

2. Remove the Bias Square and make a rotary cut along the right side of the ruler to square up the edge of the fabric. Hold the ruler down with your left hand, placing your little finger off the edge of the ruler to serve as an anchor and prevent slipping. Stand comfortably, with your head and body centered over the cutting. Do not twist your body or arm into an awkward position.

As you cut, carefully reposition your hand on the ruler to make sure the ruler doesn't shift and the markings remain accurately placed. Use firm, even pressure as you cut. Begin rolling the cutter on the mat before you reach the folded fabric edge and continue across. For safety's sake, always roll the cutter away from you. Remember that the blade is very sharp, so be careful!

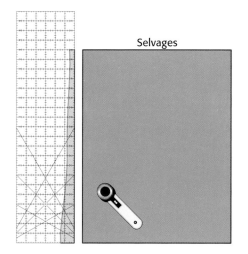

Selvages

3. Fold the fabric again so that you will be cutting 4 layers at a time. Cut strips of fabric, aligning the clean-cut edge of the fabric with the ruler markings at the desired width. Open the fabric strips periodically to make sure you are cutting straight strips. If the strips are not straight, repeat steps 1 and 2 to square up the edge of the fabric again before

cutting additional strips. Don't worry. This adjustment is common.

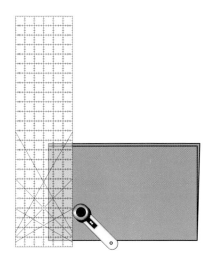

Squares and Rectangles

1. For squares, cut fabric into strips. The strips should be the same width as the finished square plus seam allowances.

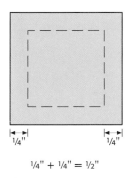

1/4"   1/4"

1/4" + 1/4" = 1/2"

2. Using the Bias Square ruler, align the top and bottom edges of each strip and cut the fabric into squares. The size of the squares is determined by the width of the strip.

3. Cut rectangles in the same manner as squares. First, use the shorter measurement of the rectangle to cut strips, then use the longer measurement to cut the strips into rectangles. Make sure your measurements include seam allowances.

4. To cut a small, odd-sized square or rectangle for which there is no marking on your ruler, make a paper template (including ¼"-wide seam allowances). Tape it to the bottom of the Bias Square, and you will have the correct alignment for cutting strips or squares.

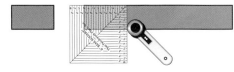

Fussy-Cut Squares

If a quilt is a scrappy quilt that uses fabric randomly, don't worry about the placement of stripes or plaids. Let them fall as they are cut, including off-grain plaids with horizontal and vertical stripes. However, if you are making a quilt that requires you to control the direction of the fabric, you will need to cut and place the pieces carefully. For example, in cutting half-square triangles from a striped fabric, cut half the triangles in one direction and the remaining triangles in the opposite direction.

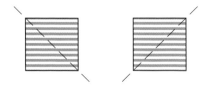

If you are sewing striped fabric to a square or diamond, place the stripes from squares cut in one direction to opposite sides of the square.

Then sew the stripes from squares cut in the opposite direction to the remaining sides of the square.

To fussy cut a design from a pictorial or theme print, use a see-through ruler and adjust the crosswise cuts to center the design.

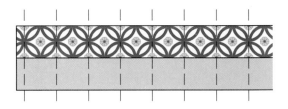

Half-Square Triangles

Most of the triangles used in the quilts in this book are half-square triangles. These triangles are cut so that the straight of grain is on the short edges of the triangles. To make these triangles, cut a square $7/8$" larger than the finished size of the short edge of the triangle to allow for seam allowances.

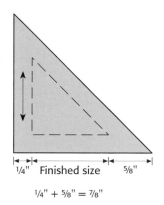

$1/4$" Finished size $5/8$"

$1/4" + 5/8" = 7/8"$

1. Cut a strip to the desired measurement.
2. Cut the strip into squares that are the same measurement as the strip width.
3. Cut a stack of these squares once diagonally.

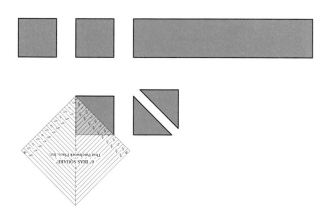

Nubbing Corners on Half-Square Triangles

Nubbing the corners on half-square triangles makes it easier to match edges precisely. Use the Bias Square ruler to trim the corners. The example shown here is a half-square triangle with a finished dimension of 4".

1. To quick-cut this triangle, cut a $47/8$" square of fabric; then cut it once diagonally.
2. To trim the corners, add $1/2$" to the finished size of the short edge. Position the Bias Square's $41/2$" mark on the fabric triangle as shown. The points of the triangle will extend $3/8$". Trim them off with the rotary cutter.

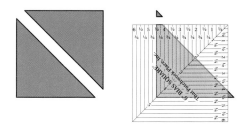

Quarter-Square Triangles

These triangles are cut so that the straight of grain is on the long edges of the triangles. The long sides are placed along the outside edges of blocks and quilts to keep the edges of quilts from stretching. Cut a square $11/4$" larger than the finished size of the long edge of the triangle to allow for seam allowances.

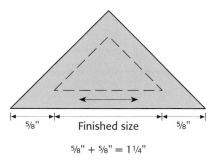

$5/8$" Finished size $5/8$"

$5/8" + 5/8" = 1 1/4"$

1. Cut a strip as wide as the desired finished measurement.
2. Cut the strip into squares that are the same measurement as the strip width.

3. Cut a stack of squares twice diagonally.

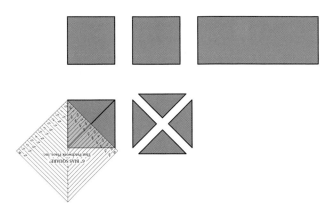

MACHINE PIECING

It's important to be comfortable with the sewing machine you are using. If this is your first machine-made quilt, practice guiding fabric through the machine. If you leave the machine unthreaded, you can practice over and over again on the same pieces of fabric.

Operating a sewing machine requires the same type of coordination it takes to drive a car. You use your foot to control the machine's speed and your hands to guide the fabric that feeds into the machine. A good habit to develop is to use a seam ripper or long pin to gently guide the fabric up to the needle. You can hold seam intersections together or make minor adjustments before the fabric is sewn.

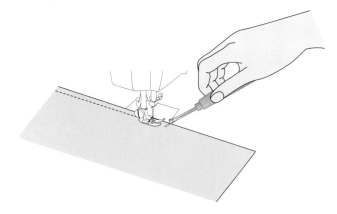

The most important skill in machine piecing is sewing an accurate ¼"-wide seam. This is necessary for seams to match and for the resulting block or quilt to measure the required size. There are several methods that will help you achieve this.

- Purchase a special foot that is sized so that you can align the edge of your fabric with the edge of the presser foot, resulting in a seam that is ¼" away from the fabric edge. Bernina has a special patchwork foot (#37), and Little Foot makes several special ¼" feet that fit most machines.
- If you have an electronic or computerized sewing machine, adjust the needle position so that the resulting seam is ¼" away from the fabric edge.
- Find the ¼"-wide seam allowance on your machine by placing an accurate template under the presser foot and lowering the needle onto the seam line. Mark the seam allowance by placing a piece of masking tape at the edge of the template. You can use several layers of masking tape, building a raised edge to guide your fabric. You can also use a piece of moleskin for a raised seam guide.

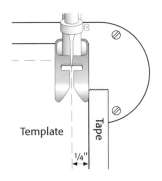

Do the following test to make sure that the method you are using results in an accurate ¼"-wide seam.

1. Cut 3 strips of fabric, each 1½" x 3".
2. Sew the strips together, using the edge of the presser foot or the seam guide you have made. Press seams toward the outer edges. After sewing and pressing, the center strip should measure exactly 1" wide. If it doesn't, adjust the needle or seam guide in the proper direction.

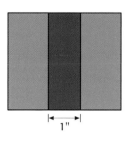

Matching Seams

When sewing the fabric pieces that make up a unit or block, follow the piecing diagram provided. Press each group of pieces before joining it to the next unit.

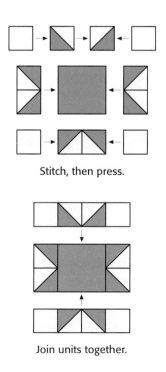

Stitch, then press.

Join units together.

There are several techniques you can use to get your seams to match perfectly.

Opposing Seams: When stitching one seamed unit to another, press seams that need to match in opposite directions. The two "opposing" seams will hold each other in place and evenly distribute the fabric bulk. Plan pressing to take advantage of opposing seams. You will find this particularly important in strip piecing.

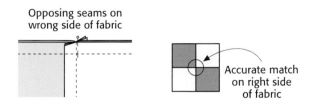

Positioning Pin: A pin, carefully pushed straight through two points that need to match and pulled tight, will establish the proper matching point. Pin the remainder of the seam normally and remove the positioning pin just before stitching.

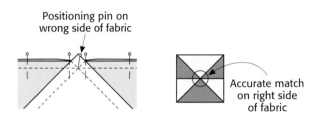

The **X**: When triangles are pieced, the stitches will form an **X** at the next seam line. Stitch through the center of the **X** to make sure the points on the sewn triangles will not be cut off.

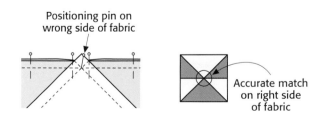

Easing: When two pieces you are sewing together are supposed to match but are slightly different in length, pin the points to match and stitch with the shorter piece on top. The feed dogs will ease the fullness of the bottom piece.

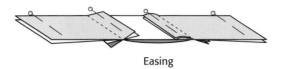

Easing

Inspect each intersection from the right side to see that it is matched. If seams do not meet accurately, note which direction the fabric needs to be moved. Use a seam ripper to rip out the seam intersection and ½" of stitching on either side of the intersection. Shift fabric to correct the alignment, place positioning pins, then restitch.

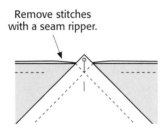

Remove stitches with a seam ripper.

Pressing: After stitching a seam, it is important to press your work. Careful pressing helps make the next steps in the stitching process, such as matching points or aligning seams, easier. Pressing arrows (——▶) are provided in many illustrations for this book when the direction in which you press the seams is important. Following these arrows will help in constructing the blocks and assembling the quilt top.

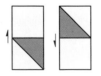

Be sure to press, not iron, your work. Ironing is an aggressive back-and-forth motion that we use on clothing to remove wrinkles. This action can easily pull and distort the bias edges or seams in your piecing. Perfectly marked and sewn quilt pieces are commonly distorted by excessive ironing. You may notice this particularly after sewing what were two perfectly marked, cut, and sewn triangles into a square. Many times the finished unit is no longer square after you've ironed it. Pressing is the gentle lowering, pressing, and lifting of the iron along the length of the fabric without moving the iron back forth along the seam. Let the heat, steam, and an occasional spritz of water press the fabric in the desired direction.

Chain Piecing

Chain piecing is an assembly-line approach to putting your blocks together. Rather than sewing each block from start to finish, you can sew identical units of each block together at one time, streamlining the process. It's a good idea, however, to first sew one sample block together from start to finish to ensure that the pieces have been accurately cut and that you have the proper positioning and coloration for each piece.

Stack the units you will be sewing in pairs, arranging any opposing seam allowances so that the top seam allowance faces toward the needle and the lower seam allowance faces toward you. Then you won't need to keep checking to see if the lower seam allowance is being pulled to the wrong side by the feed dogs as you feed the fabric through the sewing machine.

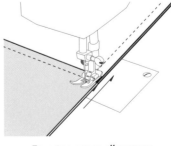

Face top seam allowance toward the needle whenever possible.

Use a "thread saver" to begin and end all your seams. Keep a stack of fabric scraps, about 2" x 2", near your machine. When you begin to sew, fold one of the squares in half and sew to its edge.

Use a thread saver
to begin sewing.

Leave the presser foot down and continue sewing onto your piecing units. Feed the units through the machine without stopping to cut thread. There will be a "stitch" or small length of thread between the units.

When you have finished chain piecing or sewing a seam, sew onto another thread saver, leaving the needle in place and the presser foot down. This thread saver will be in place for sewing the next seam or unit. This technique saves thread because you don't stop and pull a length of thread to remove the fabric from the machine. All the tails of thread will be on the thread saver and not on the back of the block or quilt. This method also keeps the machine from eating the edges of the fabric as you start a seam and can be used anytime you sew, not just when you chain piece.

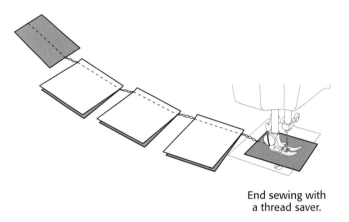

End sewing with
a thread saver.

Finally, take the connected units to the ironing board for pressing, then clip them apart. Chain piecing takes a little planning, but it saves you time and thread.

Christmas Nine Patch

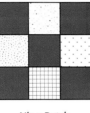

Nine Patch

Finished Quilt Size: 20¼" x 20¼"
Finished Block Size: 3" x 3"

9 blocks, set diagonally with alternating unpieced blocks and side and corner setting triangles; ½"-wide inner border; 3¼"-wide outer border

TIME-CRUNCH FEATURES

- Small Quilts (page 9)
- Theme Prints (pages 9–10)
- Blocks Set Diagonally (page 12)
- Nine Patch Blocks (pages 16–17)
- Button Tufting (page 20)

MATERIALS

42"-wide fabric

1 fat quarter of red print for Nine Patch blocks and inner border
1 fat eighth each of 4 red prints with a white background for Nine Patch blocks
½ yd. Christmas print for background and outer border
⅝ yd. fabric for backing
¼ yd. fabric for 91" of bias binding
24" x 24" piece of batting

CUTTING

All measurements include ¼"-wide seams.

From the red print, cut:
   5 strips, each 1½" x 21", for Nine Patch blocks.
   2 strips, each 1" x 13¼", for inner side border.
   2 strips, each 1" x 14¼", for inner top and bottom borders.

From each of the 4 red prints with a white background, cut:
   1 strip (4 total), 1½" x 21", for Nine Patch blocks.

From the Christmas print, cut:
   4 squares, each 3½" x 3½", for unpieced blocks.
   2 squares, each 5½" x 5½". Cut twice diagonally to make 8 side setting triangles.
   2 squares, each 3" x 3". Cut once diagonally to make 4 corner setting triangles.
   2 strips, each 3½" x 14¼", for outer side borders.
   2 strips, each 3½" x 20¼", for outer top and bottom borders.

Christmas Nine Patch by Cleo Nollette, 1998, Seattle, Washington, 20¼" x 20¼". This small Nine Patch quilt is the perfect venue for the Christmas toile fabric.

DIRECTIONS

1. Referring to "Nine Patch Blocks" on page 16, join 1½" x 21" red print and red-print-with-white-background strips to make Strip Sets 1 and 2. Crosscut Strip Set 1 into 18 segments, each 1½" wide. Crosscut Strip Set 2 into 9 segments, each 1½" wide. Join the segments to make Nine Patch blocks.

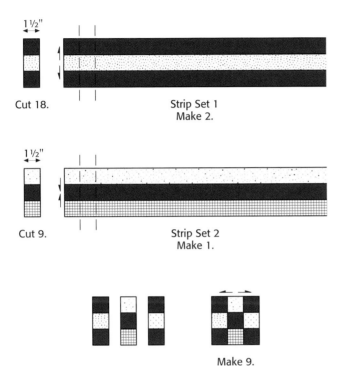

1½"

Cut 18.

Strip Set 1
Make 2.

1½"

Cut 9.

Strip Set 2
Make 1.

Make 9.

2. Join the Nine Patch blocks, unpieced blocks, and side setting triangles into diagonal rows. Join the rows. Add the corner setting triangles last.

3. Add the 1"-wide inner border strips and the 3½"-wide outer border strips, following the directions for "Straight-Cut Borders" on pages 116–117.
4. Layer the quilt top with batting and backing. Button tuft the quilt, following the directions on page 20.
5. Bind the edges with the bias strips.

Ann's Little Nine Patch (alternate quilt) by Cleo Nollette, 1999, Seattle, Washington, 20¼" x 20¼". Different fabrics make a sunny quilt that will brighten any day. Select a light background print instead of the red Christmas toile print. Use a single yellow print in the Nine Patch blocks instead of the variety of red prints, then accent with a narrow blue border.

Cake Stand

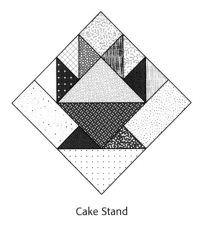

Cake Stand

Finished Quilt Size: 25½" x 25½"
Finished Block Size: 4" x 4"

9 blocks, set diagonally with alternating unpieced blocks and side and corner setting triangles; 1"-wide inner border; 3¼"-wide outer border

TIME-CRUNCH FEATURES

- Small Quilts (page 9)
- Blocks Set Diagonally (page 12)
- Bias Squares (pages 14–15)
- Button Tufting (page 20)

MATERIALS

42"-wide fabric

½ yd. total assorted red prints with white background

¼ yd. total assorted red prints for blocks

⅛ yd. red-and-white print for inner border

⅜ yd. red print for outer border

⅞ yd. fabric for backing

¼ yd. fabric for 112" of bias binding

30" x 30" piece of batting

CUTTING

All measurements include ¼"-wide seams.

From the assorted red prints with a white background, cut:

A total of 18 squares, each 2¼" x 2¼", for small bias squares.

A total of 5 squares, each 3¼" x 3¼", for large bias squares.

A total of 9 squares, 1½" x 1½", for blocks.

A total of 18 rectangles, 1½" x 2½", for blocks.

A total of 5 squares, each 2⅞" x 2⅞". Cut once diagonally to yield 10 triangles for blocks. You will only use 9.

A total of 4 squares, each 4½" x 4½", for unpieced blocks.

A total of 2 squares, each 3¾" x 3¾". Cut once diagonally to yield 4 corner setting triangles.

A total of 2 squares, each 7" x 7". Cut twice diagonally to yield 8 side setting triangles.

From the assorted red prints, cut:

A total of 18 squares, each 2¼" x 2¼", for small bias squares.

A total of 5 squares, each 3¼" x 3¼", for large bias squares.

A total of 9 squares, each 1⅞" x 1⅞". Cut once diagonally to yield 18 triangles for blocks.

Cake Stand by Cleo Nollette, 1999, Seattle, Washington, 25½" x 25½". Leftover bias squares were cut to a smaller size for this scrappy quilt.

From the red-and-white print for the inner border, cut:

2 strips, each 1½" x 17½", for sides.

2 strips, each 1½" x 19½", for top and bottom.

From the red print for the outer border, cut:

2 strips, each 3½" x 19½", for sides.

2 strips, each 3½" x 25½", for top and bottom.

DIRECTIONS

1. Draw a diagonal line on the wrong side of each 2¼" red-with-white-background square. Place a marked red-with-white-background square on top of a red square of the same size, right sides together. Sew ¼" from the drawn line on both sides. Cut on the drawn line and press the seams toward the red triangles. Trim the squares to 1½" x 1½". Place a square ruler's diagonal line on the diagonal seam and trim from all 4 sides.

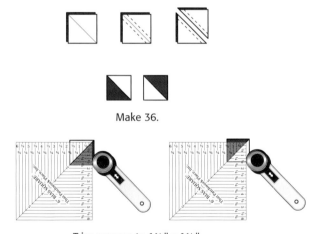

Make 36.

Trim squares to 1½" x 1½".

Note: Sewing together squares that are larger than needed and then trimming to the required size after stitching results in more accurately sized units.

2. Repeat step 1 with the 3¼" red-with-white-background squares and 3¼" red squares to make large bias squares. Trim the squares to 2½" x 2½". You will only use 9.

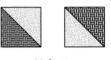

Make 9.
Trim squares to 2½" x 2½".

3. Join 4 small bias squares, 1 large bias square, and one 1½" red-with-white-background square to make the upper unit of the block

Make 9.

4. Join 2 small red triangles, 2 red-with-white-background rectangles, and 1 red-with-white-background triangle to the unit made in step 3 to complete 1 Cake Stand block.

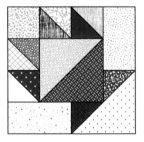

Make 9.

5. Join the Cake Stand blocks, unpieced blocks, and side setting triangles into diagonal rows. Join the rows. Add the corner setting triangles last.

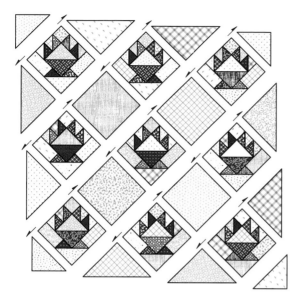

6. Add the 1½"-wide inner border strips and the 3½"-wide outer border, following the directions for "Straight-Cut Borders" on pages 116–117.

7. Layer the quilt top with batting and backing. Button tuft the quilt, following the directions on page 20.

8. Bind the edges with the bias strips.

Delectable Mountains

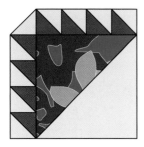

Delectable Mountains

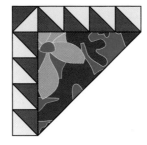

Delectable Mountains
partial block

Finished Quilt Size: 47⅝" x 47⅝"
Finished Block Size: 10"

8 blocks and 4 partial blocks surrounding a center square, set diagonally with side and corner setting triangles; 4"-wide border

TIME-CRUNCH FEATURES

- Blocks Set Diagonally (page 12)
- Bias Squares (pages 14–15)
- Easy Quilting Designs (page 19)

MATERIALS

42"-wide fabric

1¾ yds. purple print for blocks and border
1¾ yds. light blue print for background, side setting triangles, and corner setting triangles
⅜ yd. multicolored print for blocks
3 yds. fabric for backing
½ yd. fabric for 202" of bias binding
52" x 52" piece of batting

CUTTING

All measurements include ¼"-wide seams.

From the purple print, cut from the lengthwise grain:
  2 strips, each 4¼" x 40⅛", for side borders.
  2 strips, each 4¼" x 47⅝", for top and bottom borders.

From the remaining purple print, cut:
  13 squares, each 8" x 8", for bias squares.

From the light blue print, cut:
  13 squares, each 8" x 8", for bias squares.
  2 squares, each 4⅛" x 4⅛". Cut twice diagonally to yield 8 small triangles for blocks.
  4 squares, each 8⅞" x 8⅞". Cut once diagonally to yield 8 large triangles for blocks.
  1 square, 11⅞" x 11⅞", for center square.
  1 square, 12⅝" x 12⅝". Cut twice diagonally to yield 4 triangles for side setting triangles.
  2 squares, 12¼" x 12¼". Cut once diagonally to yield 4 triangles for corner setting triangles.

From the multicolored print, cut:
  6 squares, each 8⅞" x 8⅞". Cut once diagonally to yield 12 triangles for blocks.

Delectable Mountains by Cleo Nollette, 1999, Seattle, Washington, 47⅝" x 47⅝". Quilted by Martha Troyer. The bold contrast of the bright prints against the soft background creates an energized three-fabric quilt.

DIRECTIONS

1. Pair each 8" purple square with an 8" light blue square, right sides up. Cut and piece 2½"-wide bias strips, following the directions for bias squares on pages 14–15. Cut 100 bias squares, each 2½" x 2½".

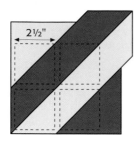

2. Join 4 bias squares to make left and right units.

Make 12.　　　　Make 12.

3. Join 1 left unit, 1 right unit, 1 small light blue triangle, 1 multicolored triangle, and 1 large light blue triangle to make a Delectable Mountains block.

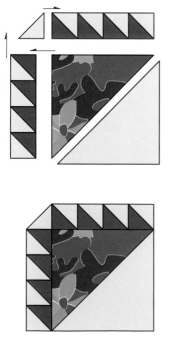

Make 8.

4. Join 1 left unit, 1 right unit, 1 bias square, and 1 multicolored triangle to make a partial block.

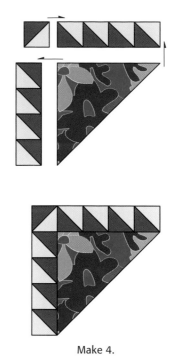

Make 4.

5. Join the partial blocks to the center square, aligning the long edge of the triangles with the sides of the square. Stitch, starting and stopping ¼" from the corners of the square; backstitch. Join the seams between the partial blocks to complete the center section.

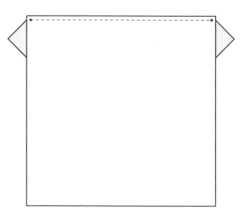

6. Join the Delectable Mountains blocks, center section, and side setting triangles into diagonal rows. Join the rows. Add the corner setting triangles last.

7. Add the 4¼"-wide border strips, referring to "Straight-Cut Borders" on pages 116–117.
8. Layer the quilt top with batting and backing. Tie or quilt as desired. See quilting suggestion below.
9. Bind the edges with bias strips.

One Union Square

One Union Square

Finished Quilt Size: 63" x 63"
Finished Block Size: 12"

9 blocks, set diagonally with alternating unpieced blocks and side and corner setting triangles; 1"-wide inner border; 5"-wide outer border

TIME-CRUNCH FEATURES

- Blocks Set Diagonally (page 12)
- Bias Squares (pages 14–15)

MATERIALS

42"-wide fabric

1 fat quarter each of 5 light prints for blocks
1 fat quarter each of 5 pink prints for blocks
1 fat quarter each of 5 green prints for blocks
2¼ yds. pink-and-green floral for blocks, unpieced blocks, corner and side setting triangles, and outer border

⅜ yd. green, pink, and white striped fabric for inner border
4 yds. fabric for backing
⅝ yd. fabric for 262" of bias binding
67" x 67" piece of batting

CUTTING

All measurements include ¼"-wide seams.

From the assorted light prints, cut:

A total of 9 squares, each 8" x 8", for bias squares.
A total of 36 squares, each 2½" x 2½", for blocks. You will need 9 sets of 4 matching squares.
A total of 9 squares, each 5¼" x 5¼". Cut twice diagonally to yield 36 background triangles for blocks.

From the assorted pink prints, cut:

A total of 9 squares, each 8" x 8", for bias squares.
A total of 9 squares, each 5¼" x 5¼". Cut twice diagonally to yield 36 accent triangles for blocks.

From the assorted green prints, cut:

A total of 18 squares, each 5¼" x 5¼". You will need 9 sets of 2 matching squares. Cut twice diagonally to yield 72 star point triangles for blocks.

One Union Square by Nancy J. Martin, 1998, Woodinville, Washington, 63" x 63". Quilted by Amanda Miller and her quilters. A soft floral serves as the perfect complement to these diagonally set blocks. This quilt was presented to Eileen Swanson to commemorate her ten years of employment at Martingale and Company.

From the pink-and-green floral print, cut from the lengthwise grain:

2 strips, each 5¼" x 53½", for outer side borders.

2 strips, each 5¼" x 63", for outer top and bottom borders.

From the remaining pink-and-green floral print, cut:

36 squares, each 2½" x 2½", for blocks.

9 squares, each 4½" x 4½", for blocks.

4 squares, each 12½" x 12½", for unpieced blocks.

2 squares, each 18¼" x 18¼". Cut twice diagonally to yield 8 side setting triangles.

2 squares, each 9⅜" x 9⅜". Cut once diagonally to yield 4 corner setting triangles.

From the green, pink, and white striped fabric, cut:

6 strips, each 1½" x 42", for inner border. Join strips end to end to make one continuous strip. From this long strip, cut 2 strips, each 1½" x 51½", for the inner side borders; and cut 2 strips, each 1½" x 53½", for the inner top and bottom borders.

DIRECTIONS

Use matching light, pink, and green fabrics for each block.

1. Pair each 8" light square with an 8" pink square, right sides up. Cut and piece 2½"-wide bias strips, following the directions for bias squares on pages 14–15. Cut 72 bias squares, each 2½" x 2½".

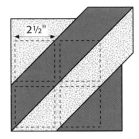

2. Join 2 bias squares, 1 light square, and 1 pink-and-green floral 2½" square to make a corner unit. Make 4 matching corner units for each block.

Corner unit
Make 4 matching units
for each block
(36 total).

3. Join 1 light triangle, 1 pink triangle, and 2 green triangles to make a side unit. Make 4 matching side units for each block.

Side unit
Make 4 matching units
for each block
(36 total).

4. Join 4 matching corner units, 4 matching side units, and 1 pink-and-green floral 4½" square to make 1 One Union Square block.

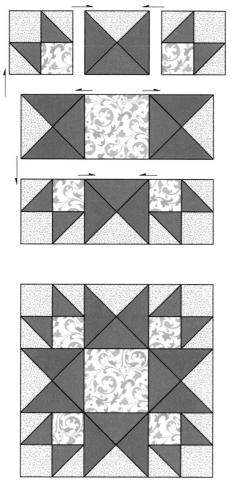

Make 9.

5. Join the One Union Square blocks, unpieced blocks, and side setting triangles in diagonal rows. Join the rows, adding the corner setting triangles last.

6. Add the 1½" inner border strips and 5¼" outer border strips, referring to "Straight-Cut Borders" on pages 116–117.
7. Layer the quilt top with batting and backing. Tie or quilt as desired. See quilting suggestion below.
8. Bind the edges with bias strips.

Norway Pine

Norway Pine

Finished Quilt Size: 57½" x 57½"
Finished Block Size: 10"

9 blocks, set diagonally with alternating unpieced blocks and side and corner setting triangles; 1"-wide inner border; 6"-wide outer border

TIME-CRUNCH FEATURES

- Blocks Set Diagonally (page 12)
- Bias Squares (pages 14–15)

MATERIALS

42"-wide fabric

1⅜ yds. off-white, tone-on-tone print for background
1¼ yds. green print #1 for blocks
1¼ yds. red print for unpieced blocks, side setting triangles, and corner setting triangles

⅜ yd. light print for inner border
1¾ yds. green print #2 for outer border
3½ yds. fabric for backing
½ yd. fabric for 242" of bias binding
62" x 62" piece of batting

CUTTING

All measurements include ¼"-wide seams.

From the off-white, tone-on-tone print, cut:
16 squares, each 8" x 8", for bias squares.
18 squares, each 2½" x 2½", for blocks.
5 squares, each 6¼" x 6¼". Cut twice diagonally to yield 20 triangles for blocks. You will only use 18.

From green print #1, cut:
16 squares, each 8" x 8", for bias squares.
9 rectangles, each 1⅞" x 5", for blocks.
5 squares, each 6⅞" x 6⅞". Cut once diagonally to yield 10 triangles for blocks. You will only use 9.

From the red print, cut:
4 squares, each 10½" x 10½", for unpieced blocks.
2 squares, each 17" x 17". Cut twice diagonally to yield 8 side setting triangles. These are cut extra large.
2 squares, each 10" x 10". Cut once diagonally to yield 4 corner setting triangles. These are cut extra large.

Norway Pine by Nancy J. Martin, 1997, Woodinville, Washington, 57½" x 57½". Quilted by the Ohio Amish. French fabrics collected on a trip to Norway add interest to this three-fabric quilt.

From the light print, cut:

5 strips, each 1½" x 42". Join strips end to end to make one continuous strip. From this long strip, cut 2 strips, each 1½" x 43½", for inner side borders; and cut 2 strips, each 1½" x 45½", for inner top and bottom borders.

From green print #2, cut:

2 strips, each 6¼" x 45½", from the lengthwise grain for outer side borders.

2 strips, each 6¼" x 57½", from the lengthwise grain for outer top and bottom borders.

DIRECTIONS

1. Pair each 8" off-white square with an 8" green print #1 square, right sides up. Cut and piece 2½"-wide bias strips, following the directions for bias squares on pages 14–15. Cut 126 bias squares, each 2½" x 2½".

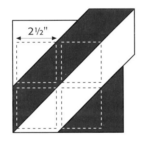

2. Join 6 bias squares to make each of the left and right sections of a block.

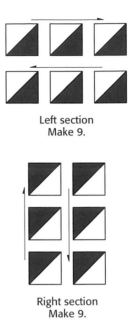

Left section
Make 9.

Right section
Make 9.

3. Join 2 bias squares and 2 off-white 2½" squares to make the top section of a block.

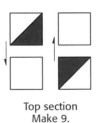

Top section
Make 9.

4. Join 2 off-white triangles and a green print #1 rectangle. Add a large green print #1 triangle. Trim the excess fabric to make a center section.

 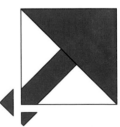

Trim excess fabric.
Make 9.

5. Join the sections to make 1 Norway Pine block.

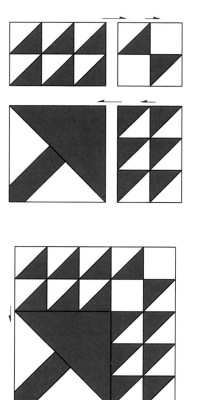

Make 9.

6. Join the Norway Pine blocks, unpieced blocks, and side setting triangles into diagonal rows. Join the rows. Add the corner setting triangles last.

7. Trim the outside edges and square up the corners of the quilt as necessary, leaving ½" of fabric outside the block corners. The quilt should measure 43½" x 43½".

8. Add the 1½"-wide inner border strips and the 6¼"-wide outer border strips, referring to "Straight-Cut Borders" on pages 116–117.

9. Layer the quilt top with batting and backing. Tie or quilt as desired. See quilting suggestion below.

10. Bind the edges with bias strips.

Sawtooth Mountains

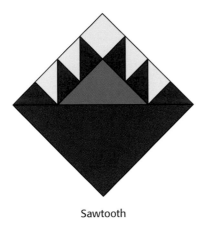

Sawtooth

Finished Quilt Size: 62¼" x 73½"
Finished Block Size: 8"

20 blocks, set diagonally with alternating unpieced blocks and side and corner triangles; 3"-wide inner border; 5½"-wide outer border

TIME-CRUNCH FEATURES

- Blocks Set Diagonally (page 12)
- Bias Squares (pages 14–15)

MATERIALS

42"-wide fabric

1 fat quarter each of 5 light prints for blocks
¾ yd. each of 6 dark prints for blocks, side setting triangles, and corner setting triangles
1 yd. yellow floral print for blocks and inner border
2 yds. paisley print for blocks and outer border
4 yds. fabric for backing (pieced crosswise)
⅝ yd. fabric for 284" of bias binding
67" x 78" piece of batting

CUTTING

All measurements include ¼"-wide seams.

From the light prints, cut:
A total of 9 squares, each 8" x 8", for bias squares.
A total of 18 squares, each 2½" x 2½", for blocks. Cut 9 sets of 2 matching squares. Make sure each set matches an 8" light-print square from above.

From the dark prints, cut:
A total of 10 squares, each 8" x 8", for bias squares.
A total of 20 squares, each 2⅞" x 2⅞". Cut 10 sets of 2 matching squares. Make sure each set matches an 8" dark-print square from above. Cut the 2⅞" squares once diagonally to yield 40 small triangles for blocks.
A total of 6 squares, each 4⅞" x 4⅞". Cut once diagonally to yield 12 medium triangles for the blocks.
A total of 8 squares, each 8⅞" x 8⅞". Cut once diagonally to yield 16 large triangles for the blocks.
A total of 10 squares, each 8½" x 8½", for alternating unpieced blocks.

From each of 3 dark prints, cut:
1 square (3 total), each 12⅝" x 12⅝". Cut twice diagonally to yield 12 side setting triangles.

Sawtooth Mountains by Nancy J. Martin, 1999, Woodinville, Washington, 62¼" x 73½". Quilted by Amanda Miller and her quilters. This lively quilt features French prints collected in Provence, France, and some classic domestic prints. The setting for this quilt was inspired by a Country Threads quilt called "Barn Dance."

From each of 2 dark prints, cut:

1 square (2 total), each 6⅝" x 6⅝". Cut once diagonally to yield 4 corner setting triangles.

From the yellow floral print, cut:

1 square, 8" x 8", for bias squares.

2 squares, each 2½" x 2½", for blocks.

2 squares, each 4⅞" x 4⅞". Cut once diagonally to yield 4 medium triangles for the blocks.

6 strips, each 3½" x 42", for inner border. Join strips end to end. From this long strip, cut 2 strips, each 3½" x 57⅛", for inner side borders; and cut 2 strips, each 3½" x 51¾", for inner top and bottom borders.

From the paisley, cut from the lengthwise grain:

2 strips, each 5¾" x 63⅛", for outer side borders.

2 strips, each 5¾" x 62 ¼", for outer top and bottom borders.

From the remaining paisley, cut:

2 squares, each 4⅞" x 4⅞". Cut once diagonally to yield 4 medium triangles for the blocks.

2 squares, each 8⅞" x 8⅞". Cut once diagonally to yield 4 large triangles for the blocks.

2 squares, each 8½" x 8½", for unpieced blocks.

1 square, 12⅝" x 12⅝". Cut twice diagonally to yield 4 side setting triangles.

DIRECTIONS

1. Pair the 8" dark squares with the 8" light squares and 8" yellow square, right sides up. Cut and piece 2½"-wide bias strips, following the directions for bias squares on pages 14–15. Cut 80 bias squares, each 2½" x 2½".

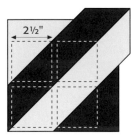

2. Join 4 bias squares, 2 small triangles, 1 medium triangle, and one 2½" square to make a unit. Use matching light and dark fabrics for each unit.

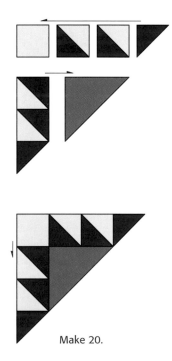

Make 20.

3. Join a large triangle to each unit made in step 2 to make 1 Sawtooth Mountains block.

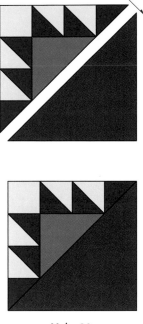

Make 20.

4. Arrange the Sawtooth Mountains blocks, unpieced blocks, and side setting triangles in diagonal rows. Join the rows, adding the corner triangles last.

5. Add the 3½"-wide inner border strips and 5¾"-wide outer border strips, referring to "Straight-Cut Borders" on pages 116–117.

6. Layer the quilt top with batting and backing. Tie or quilt as desired. See quilting suggestion below.

7. Bind the edges with bias strips.

True Blue

Corner Star

Finished Quilt Size: 63½" x 63½"
Finished Block Size: 17"

9 blocks, set 3 across and 3 down; 6¼"-wide pieced border

TIME-CRUNCH FEATURES

- Large Blocks (pages 10–11)
- Easiest Pieced Border in the World (pages 17–18)
- Easy Quilting Designs (page 19)

MATERIALS

42"-wide fabric

½ yd. each of 6 light blue prints with a white background
½ yd. each of 6 medium blue prints for blocks
⅜ yd. each of 6 navy blue prints for blocks
4 yds. fabric for backing
⅝ yd. fabric for 264" of bias binding
68" x 68" piece of batting

CUTTING

All measurements include ¼"-wide seams.

From the light blue prints with a white background, cut:

A total of 18 squares, each 5¼" x 5¼". You will need 9 sets of 2 matching squares. Cut twice diagonally to yield 72 small triangles for blocks.

A total of 9 squares, each 9⅜" x 9⅜". Cut twice diagonally to yield 36 large triangles for blocks.

A total of 9 squares, each 4½" x 4½", for blocks.

From the medium blue and navy blue prints, cut:

A total of 12 strips, each 3½" x 42", for the pieced border.

From the remaining medium blue prints, cut:

A total of 18 squares, each 5¼" x 5¼". You will need 9 sets of 2 matching squares. Cut twice diagonally to yield 72 small triangles for blocks.

A total of 36 squares, each 2½" x 2½", for blocks. You will need 9 sets of 4 matching squares. Make sure each set matches 1 of the 9 sets of medium blue triangles from above.

True Blue by Nancy J. Martin, 1999, Woodinville, Washington, 63½" x 63½". Quilted by Fannie Yoder. Favorite blue fabrics create a calm, restful quilt. The straight-line quilting in the alternate blocks can be done quickly.

From the remaining navy blue prints, cut:

A total of 36 rectangles, each 2½" x 4½", for blocks. You will need 9 sets of 4 matching rectangles.

A total of 36 squares, each 2½" x 2½", for blocks. You will need 9 sets of 4 matching squares. Make sure each set matches 1 of the 9 sets of rectangles from above.

From each of 4 navy blue prints, cut:

1 square (4 total), 3½" x 3½", for corner squares.

1 rectangle (4 total), 3½" x 6½", for corner squares.

From each of 4 medium blue prints, cut:

1 square (4 total), 3½" x 3½", for corner squares.

DIRECTIONS

Note: Use matching light blue-with-white-background triangles, medium blue pieces, and navy blue pieces for each block.

1. Join a 2½" x 4½" navy blue rectangle, a 2½" navy blue square, and a 2½" medium blue square to make a corner unit. Make 4 matching units for each block.

Corner unit
Make 4 matching units
for each block (36 total).

2. Join 2 small light-blue triangles and 2 small medium-blue triangles to make a side unit. Make 4 matching units for each block.

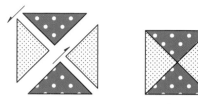

Side unit
Make 4 matching units
for each block (36 total).

3. Join 4 matching corner units, 4 matching side units, and one 4½" light-blue square to make 1 star unit.

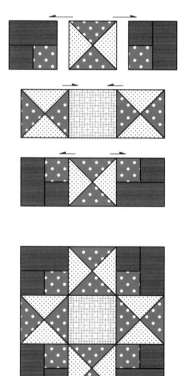

Make 9.

4. Join 4 matching large, light-blue triangles to each star unit to make 1 Corner Star block.

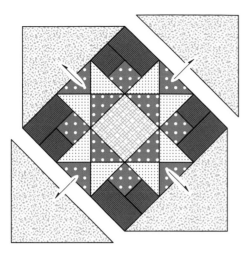

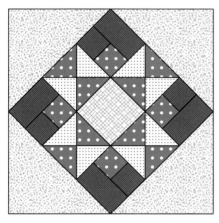

Make 9.

5. Join the blocks in 3 rows of 3 blocks each. Join the rows.

6. Join the 3½"-wide blue strips to make 2 strip units of 6 strips each. Crosscut the strip sets into 12 segments, each 6½" wide.

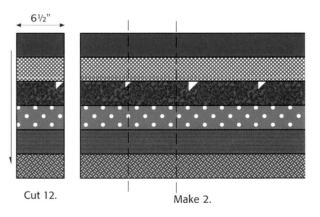

6½"

Cut 12.

Make 2.

7. Join 3 segments from step 6 end to end to make each of the 4 borders. Remove one strip from each border.

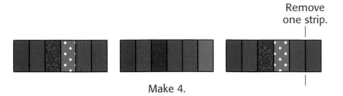

Remove one strip.

Make 4.

8. Join a 3½" x 6½" navy blue rectangle, a 3½" matching navy blue square, and a 3½" medium blue square to make a pieced corner square.

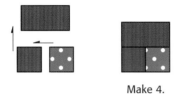

Make 4.

9. Join pieced borders to the sides of the quilt top. Add a pieced corner square to each end of the remaining pieced borders. Add these to the top and bottom edges of the quilt.

10. Layer the quilt top with batting and backing. Tie or quilt as desired. See quilting suggestion below.

11. Bind the edges with bias strips.

Lady of the Lake

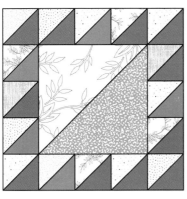

Lady of the Lake

Finished Quilt Size: 82½" x 82½"
Finished Block Size: 12½"

16 blocks, set 4 across and 4 down with 2½"-wide sashing; 10"-wide border

TIME-CRUNCH FEATURES

- Large Blocks (pages 10–11)
- Bias Squares (pages 14–15)

MATERIALS

42"-wide fabric

½ yd. each of 4 light prints for blocks
½ yd. each of 4 dark prints for blocks
1 yd. light floral print for blocks and corner squares
2⅜ yds. dark floral print for blocks and border
1⅜ yds. dark print for sashing
7¼ yds. fabric for backing
¾ yds. fabric for 340" of bias binding
87" x 87" piece of batting

CUTTING

All measurements include ¼"-wide seams.

From each of the 4 light prints, cut:
9 squares (36 total), each 8" x 8", for bias squares.

From each of the 4 dark prints, cut:
9 squares (36 total), each 8" x 8", for bias squares.

From the light floral print, cut:
8 squares, each 8⅜" x 8⅜". Cut once diagonally to yield 16 triangles for blocks.
4 squares, each 10¼" x 10¼", for corner squares.

From the dark floral print, cut from the lengthwise grain:
4 strips, each 10¼" x 63", for border.

From the remaining dark floral print, cut:
8 squares, each 8⅜" x 8⅜". Cut once diagonally to yield 16 triangles for blocks.

From the dark print for sashing, cut:
14 strips, each 3" x 42". Crosscut the strips into 40 segments, each 3" x 13".

DIRECTIONS

1. Pair each 8" light-print square with an 8" dark-print square, right sides up. Cut and piece 2¾"-wide bias strips, following the directions for bias squares on pages 14–15. Cut 281 bias squares, each 3" x 3".

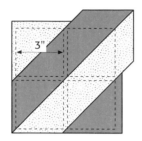

2. Join 1 light floral triangle and 1 dark floral triangle to make a center unit.

Make 16.

3. Join 16 bias squares and 1 center unit to make 1 Lady of the Lake block.

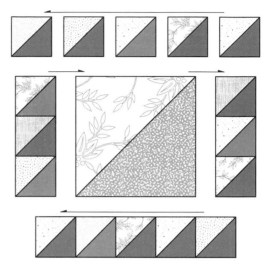

4. Join 4 blocks and 5 sashing strips to make 1 row. Make 4 rows.

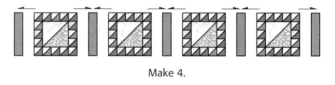

Make 4.

5. Join 4 sashing strips and 5 bias squares to make 1 sashing row. Make 5 sashing rows.

Make 5.

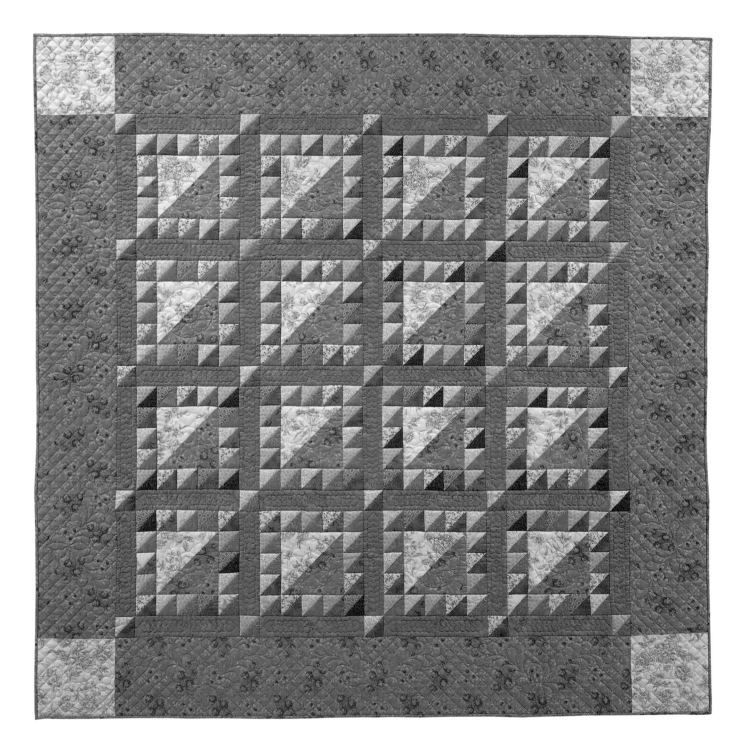

Lady of the Lake by Nancy J. Martin, 1999, Woodinville, Washington, 82½" x 82½". Quilted by Alvina Nelson. Soft shades of sage green are bordered by a romantic print for this quilt, the perfect wedding gift for my son and his bride. (Collection of Michael and Terry Martin.)

6. Join the rows of blocks and sashing.

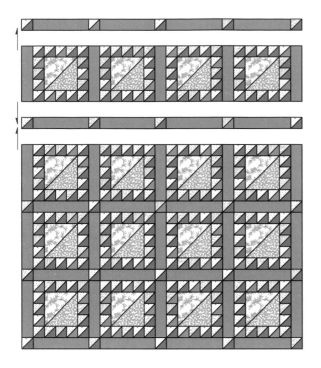

7. Join the 10¼" border strips to the sides of the quilt top, referring to "Borders with Corner Squares" on page 117. Add a corner square to each end of the remaining border strips, and add these to the top and bottom edges of the quilt.

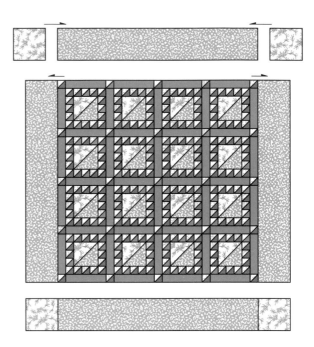

8. Layer the quilt top with batting and backing. Tie or quilt as desired. See quilting suggestion at right.

9. Bind the edges with bias strips.

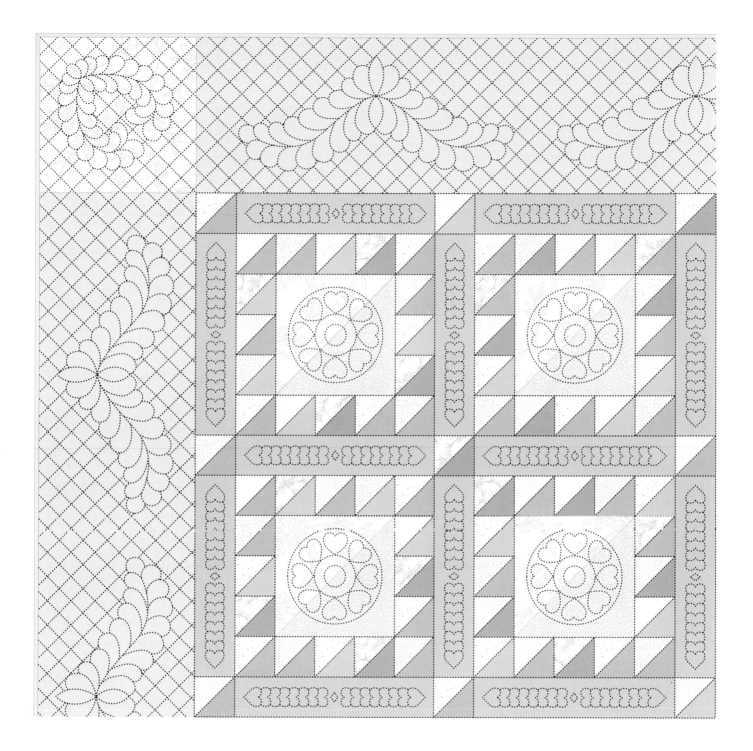

Simple Stars

Star

Finished Quilt Size: 48½" x 48½"
Finished Block Size: 14"

9 blocks, set 3 across and 3 down; 3 rounds of 1"-wide borders

TIME-CRUNCH FEATURES

- Large Blocks (pages 10–11)
- Courthouse Steps Border (page 18)

MATERIALS

42"-wide fabric

¼ yd. each of 9 navy blue prints for blocks and borders
¼ yd. each of 9 red prints for blocks and borders
⅛ yd. each of 6 light prints for background
3 yds. fabric for backing
½ yd. fabric for 204" of bias binding
53" x 53" piece of batting

CUTTING

All measurements include ¼"-wide seams.

Note: Star blocks in the quilt on the facing page were made in several different color combinations. Using desired fabrics, cut pieces for each Star block as follows:

PIECE	NO. TO CUT	DIMENSIONS
1—star points	4	2⅞" x 2⅞" ◻
2—background triangles	1	5¼" x 5¼" ⊠
3—background squares	4	2½" x 2½"
4—center square	1	4½" x 4½"

◻ = cut squares once diagonally
⊠ = cut squares twice diagonally

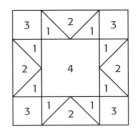

From each of the red prints, cut:
  2 strips (18 total), each 1½" x 8½", for log 1.
  2 strips (18 total), each 1½" x 10½", for log 3.
  2 strips (18 total), each 1½" x 12½", for log 5.

Simple Stars by Nancy J. Martin, 1999, Woodinville, Washington, 48½" x 48½". Quilted by Mary Hershberger. The Courthouse Steps block is used to enlarge each star and to expand the border.

From each of 6 red prints, cut:
2 strips (12 total), each 1½" x 42", for borders.

From each of the navy blue prints, cut:
2 strips (18 total), each 1½" x 10½", for log 2.
2 strips (18 total), each 1½" x 12½", for log 4.
2 strips (18 total), each 1½" x 14½", for log 6.

From each of 6 navy blue prints, cut:
2 strips (12 total), each 1½" x 42", for borders.

DIRECTIONS

1. Join 8 star points, 4 background triangles, four 2½" squares, and 1 center square to make 1 Star block. Use matching light triangles and squares, and matching dark points in each block.

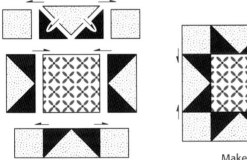

Make 9.

2. Add the logs around the Star blocks in numerical order. Choose fabrics randomly to create a scrappy look.

3. Join the blocks in 3 rows of 3 blocks each. Join the rows.

4. Piecing strips as necessary, add the red-print and blue-print border pieces to the quilt top in numerical order. Alternate red strips on the sides and blue strips on the top and bottom edges. Refer to "Straight-Cut Borders" on pages 116–117 for measuring the quilt top.

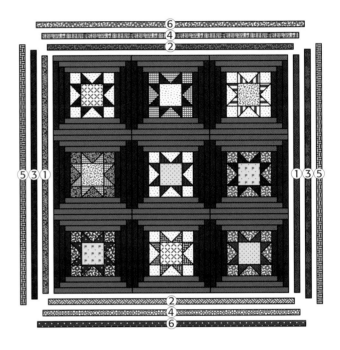

5. Layer the quilt top with batting and backing. Tie or quilt as desired. See quilting suggestion below.

6. Bind the edges with bias strips.

It's A Good Sign

Autograph

Finished Quilt Size: 55¾" x 72"
Finished Block Size: 12¾"

12 blocks, set 3 across and 4 down with 3½"-wide sashing; 1¾"-wide border

TIME-CRUNCH FEATURE

• Wide Sashing (page 11)

MATERIALS

42"-wide fabric

⅛ yd. each of 9 dark prints for blocks
¼ yd. each of 9 light prints for blocks
⅛ yd. muslin for blocks
1⅝ yds. fabric for sashing
½ yd. fabric for outer border
3½ yds. fabric for backing (pieced crosswise)
⅝ yd. fabric for 266" of bias binding
60" x 76" piece of batting

CUTTING

All measurements include ¼"-wide seams.

From each of the 9 dark prints, cut:
8 squares (72 total), each 3½" x 3½", for blocks.

From each of the 9 light prints, cut:
4 squares (36 total), each 3½" x 3½", for blocks.
2 squares (18 total), each 5½" x 5½". Cut twice diagonally to yield 72 triangles for block side setting triangles.
2 squares (18 total), each 3" x 3". Cut once diagonally to yield 36 triangles for block corner setting triangles.

From the muslin, cut:
9 squares, each 3½" x 3½", for blocks.

From the fabric for sashing, cut:
4 strips, each 4" x 52¾", for horizontal sashing strips.
16 rectangles, each 4" x 13¼", for vertical sashing strips.

From the fabric for outer border, cut:
7 strips, each 2" x 42", for outer borders. Join strips end to end to make one continuous strip. From this long strip, cut 2 strips, each 2" x 69", for side borders; and cut 2 strips, each 2" x 55¾", for top and bottom borders.

DIRECTIONS

1. Join 8 dark squares, 4 light squares, 1 muslin square, and 8 light side setting triangles in diagonal rows. Join the rows and add the light corner setting triangles to complete 1 Autograph block. Use matching dark squares and matching light pieces in each block.

Make 12.

2. Join 3 blocks and 4 vertical sashing strips to make 1 row. Make 4 rows.

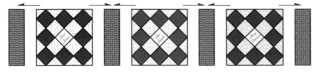

Make 4.

3. Join the rows of blocks and horizontal sashing strips.

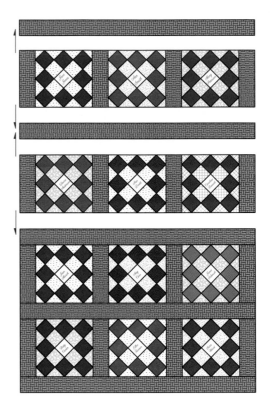

4. Add the 2"-wide outer border, referring to "Straight-Cut Borders" on pages 116–117.
5. Layer the quilt top with batting and backing. Tie or quilt as desired. See quilting suggestion below.
6. Bind the edges with bias strips.

It's a Good Sign by Nancy J. Martin and Cleo Nollette, 1999, Woodinville, Washington, 55¾" x 72". Quilted by MaryAnn Yoder. The wide sashing, cut from a bold plaid-and-floral print, highlights a traditional Autograph block.

Doves in the Window

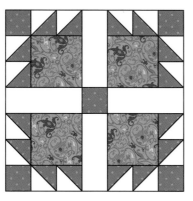

Doves in the Window

Finished Quilt Size: 82" x 82"
Finished Block Size: 14"

9 blocks, set 3 across and 3 down with 5½"-wide sashing; 10"-wide border

TIME-CRUNCH FEATURES

- Wide Sashing (page 11)
- Bias Squares (pages 14–15)

MATERIALS

42"-wide fabric

½ yd. each of 5 green prints with a white background for blocks
¼ yd. each of 9 medium green prints for blocks
1⅞ yds. fabric for sashing
⅝ yd. fabric for sashing squares
2½ yds. fabric for border
7½ yds. fabric for backing
¾ yd. fabric for 338" of bias binding
86" x 86" piece of batting

CUTTING

All measurements include ¼"-wide seams.

Note: The blocks in the quilt on the facing page were made in several different color combinations. Using desired fabrics, cut pieces for each block as follows:

Piece No.	Fabric	No. of Pieces	Dimensions
1	Green with white background	2	8" x 8" (See step 1.)
1	Medium green	2	8" x 8" (See step 1.)
2	Medium green	5	2½" x 2½"
3	Medium green	4	4½" x 4½"
4	Green with white background	4	2½" x 6½"

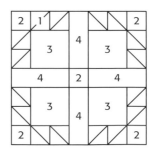

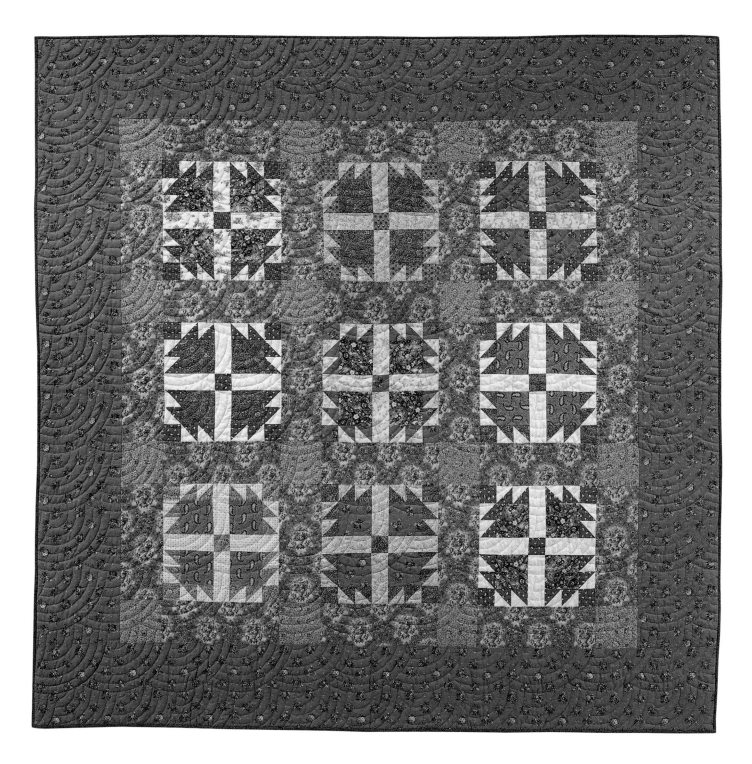

Doves in the Window by Nancy J. Martin, 1999, Woodinville, Washington, 82" x 82". Quilted by Irene Schwartz. A fabric with stylized urns of flowers was selected for the wide sashing in this quilt. The fabric was carefully cut so that all the urns are right side up.

From the fabric for the sashing, cut:
4 strips, each 14½" x 42". Cut the strips into 24 rectangles, each 5½" x 14½".

From the fabric for the sashing squares, cut:
3 strips, each 5½" x 42". Cut the strips into 16 squares, each 5½" x 5½".

From the fabric for the border, cut from the lengthwise grain:
2 strips, each 10¼" x 62½", for side borders.
2 strips, each 10¼" x 82", for top and bottom borders.

DIRECTIONS

1. Pair each 8" background square with an 8" medium green square, right sides up. Cut and piece 2½"-wide bias strips, following the directions for bias squares on pages 14–15. Cut 8 bias squares, each 2½" x 2½", from each pair of squares. You will need 16 matching bias squares for each block.

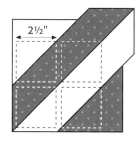

2. Join 4 matching bias squares, 1 medium green 2½" square that matches the bias squares, and 1 medium green 4½" square to make a corner unit. Make 4 matching corner units for each block.

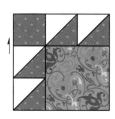
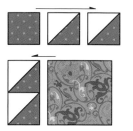

Corner unit
Make 4 matching units
for each block (36 total).

3. Join 4 matching corner units, 4 matching green-with-white-background rectangles, and 1 medium green 2½" square that matches the bias squares to make 1 Doves in the Window block.

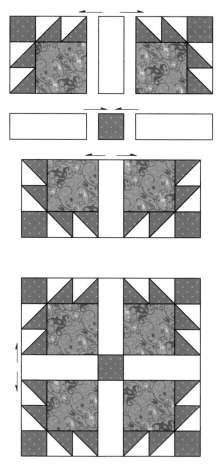

Make 9.

4. Join 3 blocks and 4 sashing strips to make 1 row. Make 3 rows.

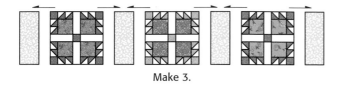

Make 3.

5. Join 3 sashing strips and 4 sashing squares to make 1 row. Make 4 rows.

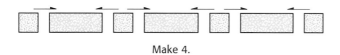

Make 4.

6. Join the rows of blocks and sashing.

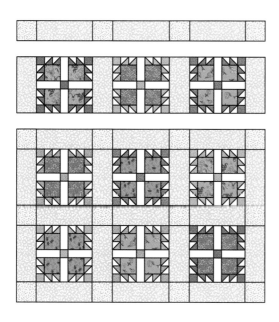

7. Add the 10¼"-wide border, referring to "Straight-Cut Borders" on pages 116–117.

8. Layer the quilt top with batting and backing. Tie or quilt as desired. See quilting suggestion below.

9. Bind the edges with bias strips.

Wasting Away in Margaritaville

One Union Square

Finished Quilt Size: 61" x 61"
Finished Block Size: 12"

9 blocks, set 3 across and 3 down with 3½"-wide sashing and sashing squares; 5½"-wide border

TIME-CRUNCH FEATURES

• Wide Sashing (page 11)
• Bias Squares (pages 14–15)

MATERIALS

42"-wide fabric

¼ yd. theme print* for block centers
¼ yd. each of 12 assorted pink, purple, turquoise, and green prints for blocks and sashing
½ yd. yellow print #1 for blocks
1⅞ yds. yellow print #2 for blocks, sashing, and border
3¾ yds. fabric for backing
½ yd. fabric for 254" of bias binding
65" x 65" piece of batting

* You may need additional yardage if you want to center specific design motifs within each square.

CUTTING

All measurements include ¼"-wide seams. Use Templates A and B on page 80.

Note: The blocks in the quilt on the facing page were made in several different color combinations. Using desired fabrics, cut pieces for each block as follows:

Piece No.	No. of Pieces	Dimensions
1–bias squares	8	(See step 1.)
2–background squares	4	2½" x 2½"
3–inner squares	4	2½" x 2½"
4–star tips	2	5¼" x 5¼" ⊠
5–background triangles	1	5¼" x 5¼" ⊠
6–accent triangles	1	5¼" x 5¼" ⊠
7–center square	1	4½" x 4½"

⊠ = cut squares twice diagonally

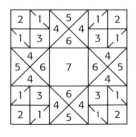

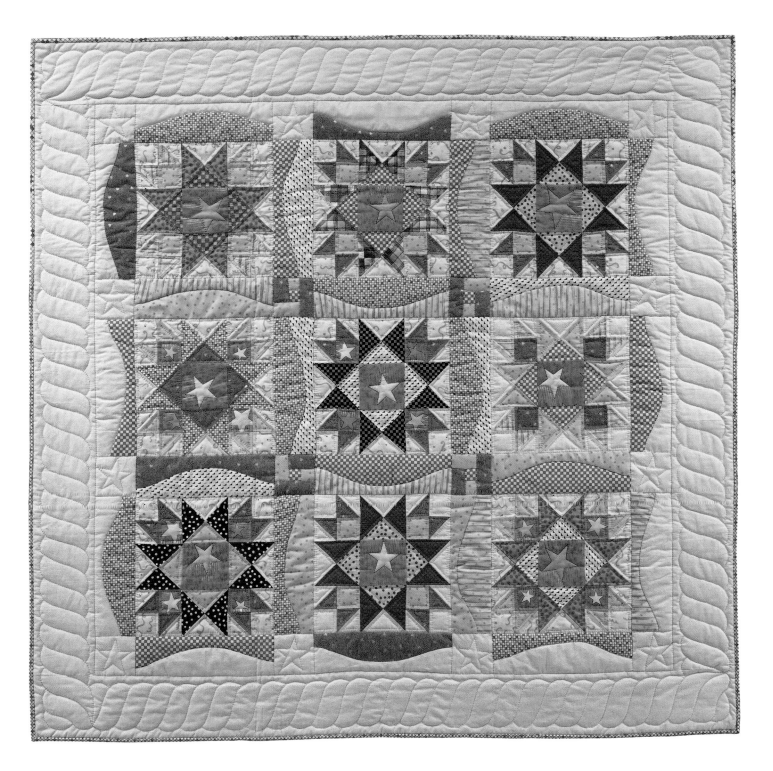

Wasting Away in Margaritaville by Nancy J. Martin, 1999, Woodinville, Washington, 61" x 61". Quilted by Fannie Yoder Millersburg. The curved, pieced sashing creates a feeling of movement across the quilt.

From the assorted prints, cut:

A total of 9 squares, each 8" x 8", for bias squares.

A total of 18 of Template A for pieced sashing.

A total of 18 of Template B for pieced sashing.

From yellow print #1, cut:

5 squares, each 8" x 8", for bias squares.

From yellow print #2, cut from the lengthwise grain:

2 strips, each 5¾" x 50½", for side borders.

2 strips, each 5¾" x 61", for top and bottom borders.

From the remaining yellow print #2, cut:

4 squares, each 8" x 8", for bias squares.

6 of Template A for pieced sashing.

6 of Template B for pieced sashing.

12 squares, each 4" x 4", for outer sashing squares.

DIRECTIONS

1. Pair each 8" yellow-print square with an 8" assorted-print square, right sides up. Cut and piece 2½"-wide bias strips, following the directions for bias squares on pages 14–15. Cut 72 bias squares, each 2½" x 2½".

2. Join 2 bias squares, 1 inner square, and 1 background square to make a corner unit. Make 4 matching corner units for each block.

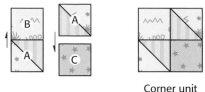

Corner unit
Make 4 matching units
for each block
(36 total).

3. Join 1 accent triangle, 1 background triangle, and 2 star tips to make a side unit. Make 4 matching side units for each block.

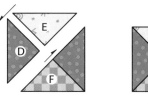

Side unit
Make 4 matching units
for each block
(36 total).

4. Join 1 center square, 4 matching corner units, and 4 matching side units to make 1 One Union Square block.

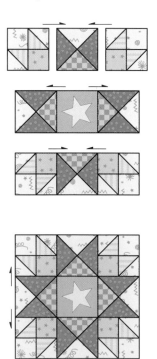

Make 9.

5. Join Template A and B pieces, right sides together, to make the following sashing units. With Piece A on top, pin the ends and the centers. Add pins as necessary to ease the curves together. Stitch. Press the seam toward Template A.

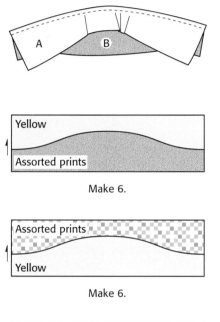

Make 6.

Make 6.

Make 12.

6. From the assorted fabrics, cut the following for the pieced sashing squares:

   4 squares, each 1½" x 1½".
   4 rectangles, 1½" x 1¾".
   8 rectangles, each 1¾" x 2¾".
   4 rectangles, each 1¾" x 4".

7. Join the squares and rectangles from step 6 to make 4 pieced sashing squares.

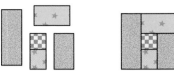

Make 4.

8. Join the blocks, pieced sashing strips, yellow sashing squares, and pieced sashing squares into rows. Join the rows.

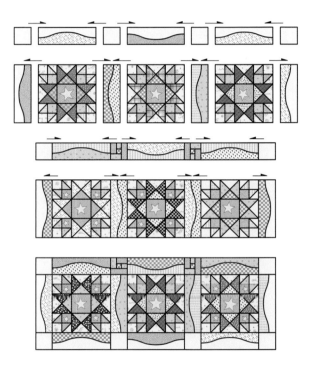

9. Add the 5¾"-wide border strips, referring to "Straight-Cut Borders" on pages 116–117.

10. Layer the quilt top with batting and backing. Tie or quilt as desired. See quilting suggestion at right.

11. Bind the edges with bias strips.

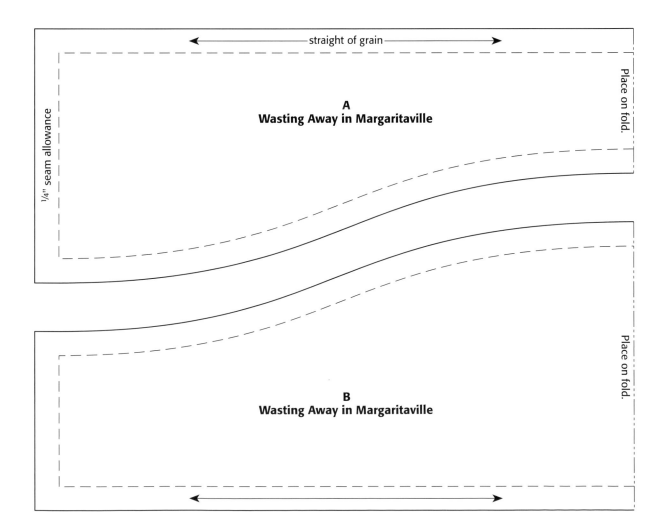

straight of grain

¼" seam allowance

Place on fold.

A
Wasting Away in Margaritaville

Place on fold.

B
Wasting Away in Margaritaville

Nine Patch Stars

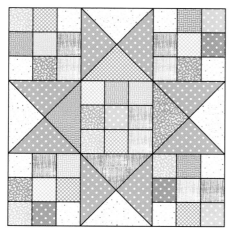

Nine Patch Star

Finished Quilt Size: 76" x 76"
Finished Block Size: 13½"

25 blocks, set 5 across and 5 down; ¾"-wide inner border, 3½"-wide outer border

TIME-CRUNCH FEATURES

• Two Alternating Blocks (page 13)
• Nine Patch Blocks (pages 16–17)

MATERIALS

42"-wide fabric

2⅜ yds. light print for pieced blocks and unpieced blocks

1 fat quarter each of 8 assorted green prints for block

1 fat quarter each of 8 assorted pink prints for blocks

1 fat quarter each of 8 assorted yellow prints for blocks

⅜ yd. pink print for inner border
1⅛ yds. green print for blocks and outer border
4⅝ yds. fabric for backing
⅝ yd. fabric for 314" of bias binding
80" x 80" piece of batting

CUTTING

All measurements include ¼"-wide seams.

From the light print, cut:
   11 strips, each 2" x 21", for nine-patch units
   13 squares, each 5¾" x 5¾". Cut twice diagonally to yield 52 triangles for blocks.
   12 squares, each 13½" x 13½", for unpieced blocks.

From the assorted green fat quarters, cut:
   A total of 24 squares, each 5¾" x 5¾". You will need 12 sets of 2 matching squares. Cut twice diagonally to yield 96 triangles for blocks.
   A total of 7 strips, each 2" x 21", for nine-patch units.

From the assorted pink fat quarters, cut:
   A total of 13 squares, each 5¾" x 5¾". Cut twice diagonally to yield 52 triangles for blocks.
   A total of 23 strips, each 2" x 21", for nine-patch units
   48 squares, each 2" x 2", for unpieced blocks.

From the assorted yellow fat quarters, cut:

A total of 25 strips, each 2" x 21", for nine-patch units.

From the pink print for inner border, cut:

7 strips, each 1¼" x 42", for inner border. Join strips end to end to make one continuous strip. From this long strip, cut 2 strips, each 1¼" x 68", for inner side borders; and cut 2 strips, each 1¼" x 69½", for inner top and bottom borders.

From the green print for blocks and outer border, cut:

2 squares, each 5¾" x 5¾". Cut twice diagonally to yield 8 triangles for blocks.

8 strips, each 3¾" x 42", for outer border. Join strips end to end to make one continuous strip. From this long strip, cut 2 strips, each 3¾" x 69½", for outer side borders; and cut 2 strips, each 3¾" x 76", for outer top and bottom borders.

DIRECTIONS

1. Referring to directions on pages 16–17 for making Nine Patch blocks, join 2" x 21" green, pink, yellow, and light strips in groups of 3 to make Strip Sets 1, 2, 3, and 4. Crosscut the strip sets into 2"-wide segments as indicated.

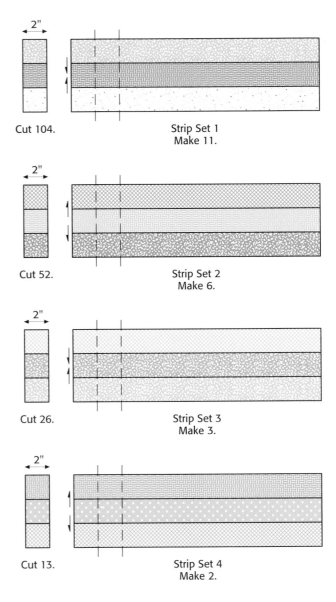

2"

Cut 104.

Strip Set 1
Make 11.

2"

Cut 52.

Strip Set 2
Make 6.

2"

Cut 26.

Strip Set 3
Make 3.

2"

Cut 13.

Strip Set 4
Make 2.

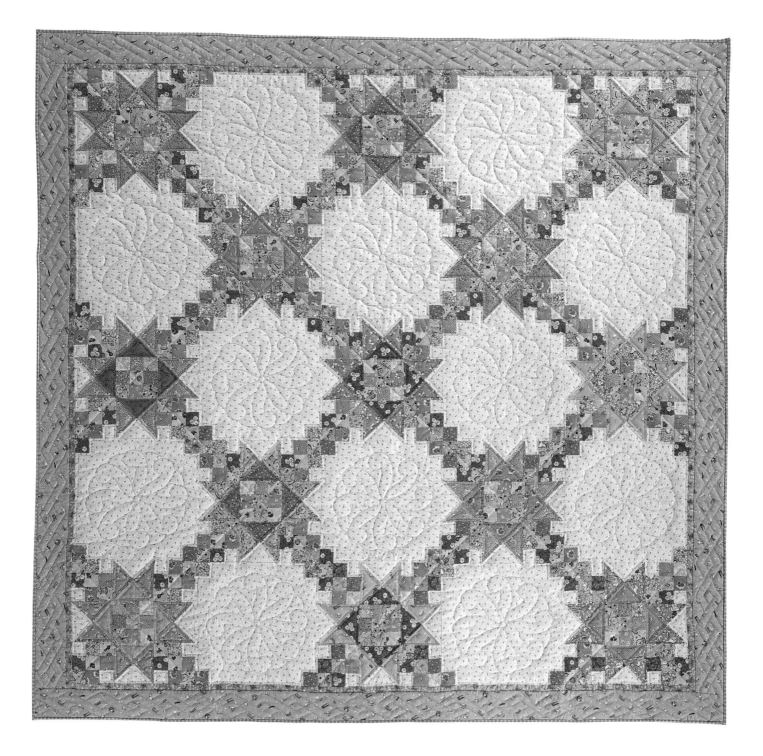

Nine Patch Stars by Nancy J. Martin, 1997, Woodinville, Washington, 76" x 76". Quilted by Bertha Stutzman. Cheerful 1930s reproduction fabrics form a chain, linked by stars, across the quilt top.

2. Join segments from Strip Sets 1 and 2 to make Unit A, and segments from Strip Sets 3 and 4 to make Unit B.

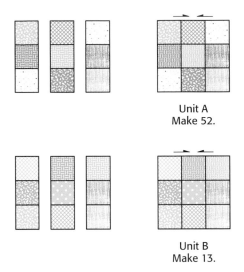

Unit A
Make 52.

Unit B
Make 13.

3. Join 1 light triangle, 1 pink triangle, and 2 green triangles to make a side unit. Make 4 matching side units for each block.

Side unit
Make 4 matching units
for each block (52 total).

4. Join 4 Unit A, 1 Unit B, and 4 matching side units to make 1 Nine Patch Stars block.

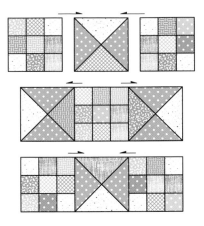

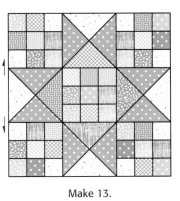

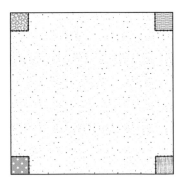

Make 13.

5. Turn under ¼" on two sides of each 2" pink square; press. Machine appliqué or hand stitch the folded edges of a pink square on each corner of the 13½" light-print squares. Align the raw edges of the pink square with the corner of the large square.

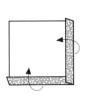

6. Join the Nine Patch Star blocks and unpieced blocks in 5 rows of 5 blocks each. Join the rows.

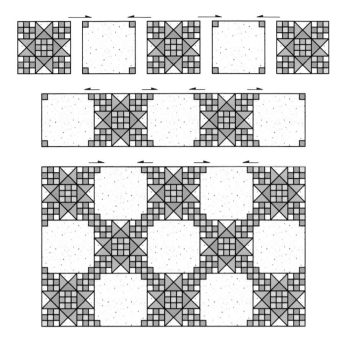

7. Add the 1¼"-wide inner border and the 3¾"-wide outer border, referring to "Straight-Cut Borders" on pages 116–117.
8. Layer the quilt top with batting and backing. Tie or quilt as desired. See quilting suggestion below.
9. Bind the edges with bias strips.

Maple Star Chain

Maple Star

Star Chain

Finished Quilt Size: 57" x 57"
Finished Block Sizes: 12"

9 blocks, set 3 across and 3 down; 1¾"-wide inner border; 8¾"-wide outer border

TIME-CRUNCH FEATURE

• Two Alternating Blocks (page 13)

MATERIALS

42"-wide fabric

½ yd. white solid fabric for Maple Star and Star Chain blocks

½ yd. floral print with white background for Maple Star and Star Chain blocks*

¼ yd. red print #1 for Maple Star blocks

¼ yd. red print #2 for Star Chain blocks

¼ yd. blue print #1 for Maple Star blocks

⅞ yd. blue print #2 for Maple Star blocks and inner border

¼ yd. blue print #3 for Star Chain blocks

¼ yd. blue-and-red print for Star Chain blocks

1¾ yds. floral border print for outer border

3½ yds. fabric for backing

½ yd. fabric for 238" of bias binding

61" x 61" piece of batting

* You may need additional yardage if you want to center specific design motifs within each square.

CUTTING

All measurements include ¼"-wide seams

From the white solid fabric, cut:

20 squares, each 2⅞" x 2⅞". Cut once diagonally to yield 40 triangles for Maple Star blocks.

4 squares, each 5¼" x 5¼". Cut twice diagonally to yield 16 triangles for Star Chain blocks.

Maple Star Chain by Nancy J. Martin, 1999, Woodinville, Washington, 57" x 57". Quilted by Elsie Raber. Two alternate pieced blocks, stitched in bright colors, are bordered with a printed stripe fabric.

From the floral print with white background, cut:
　5 squares, each 4½" x 4½", for center square of Maple Star blocks.
　16 rectangles, each 2½" x 8½", for Star Chain blocks.

From red print #1, cut:
　20 squares, each 2½" x 2½", for Maple Star blocks.

From red print #2, cut:
　32 squares, each 2½" x 2½", for Star Chain blocks.

From blue print #1, cut:
　20 rectangles, each 2½" x 4½", for Maple Star blocks.

From blue print #2, cut:
　20 squares, each 2½" x 2½", for Maple Star blocks.
　20 rectangles, each 2½" x 4½", for Maple Star blocks.
　5 squares, each 5¼" x 5¼". Cut twice diagonally to yield 20 triangles for Maple Star blocks.
　2 strips, each 2¼" x 36½", for inner side borders.
　2 strips, each 2¼" x 40", for inner top and bottom borders.

From blue print #3, cut:
　16 squares, each 2⅞" x 2⅞". Cut once diagonally to yield 32 triangles for Star Chain blocks.

From the blue-and-red print, cut:
　4 squares, each 4½" x 4½", for center squares of Star Chain blocks.

From the floral border print, cut:
　4 strips, for outer border. Strip width is equal to the width of your border design, plus ½" for seam allowances. Strip length is estimated finished quilt size (including borders), plus 3" (see page 118).

DIRECTIONS

Maple Star Blocks

1. Join a red print #1 square, a blue print #2 square, and a blue print #2 rectangle to make a corner unit.

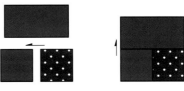

Corner unit
Make 20.

2. Join 2 white triangles and a blue print #2 triangle. Add a blue print #1 rectangle to make a side unit.

Side unit
Make 20.

3. Join 4 corner units, 4 side units, and 1 center square to make 1 Maple Star block.

(right column image)

Make 5.

Star Chain Blocks

4. Join 2 triangles from blue print #3 and a white triangle to make a star point unit.

Make 16.

5. Join 4 star point units, 4 squares from red print #2, and 1 center square to make a center star section.

Make 4.

6. Join 4 squares from red print #2, 4 floral-with-white-background rectangles, and a center star section to make 1 Star Chain block.

Make 4.

7. Join the Maple Star and Star Chain blocks in 3 rows of 3 blocks each. Join the rows.

8. Add the 2¼"-wide inner border, referring to "Straight-Cut Borders" on pages 116–117.

9. Add the outer border, referring to "Borders with Mitered Corners" on pages 117–118.

10. Layer the quilt top with batting and backing. Tie or quilt as desired. See quilting suggestion below.

11. Bind the edges with bias strips.

Woodland Spring

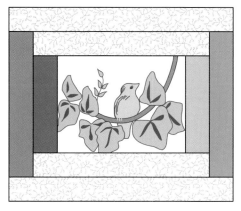

Courthouse Steps

Finished Quilt Size: 28" x 31"
Finished Block Size: 7" x 6"

12 blocks, set 3 across and 4 down; ½"-wide inner border, 3"-wide outer border

TIME-CRUNCH FEATURES

• Theme Prints (pages 9–10)
• Two Alternating Blocks (page 13)

MATERIALS

42"-wide fabric

¾ yd. theme print for blocks and inner border*
1 fat eighth each of 4 green prints for blocks
½ yd. green print for outer border
1 yd. fabric for backing
¼ yd. fabric for 128" of bias binding
32" x 35" piece of batting

* You may need additional yardage if you want to center specific design motifs within each rectangle.

CUTTING

All measurements include ¼"-wide seams.

From the theme print, cut:
> 12 rectangles, each 3½" x 4½", for blocks.
> 7 strips, each 1¼" x 42", for blocks.
> 2 strips, each 1" x 24½", for inner side borders.
> 2 strips, each 1" x 22½", for inner top and bottom borders.

From each of the green fat eighths, cut:
> 4 strips, 1¼" x 21", for blocks.

From the green print for the outer border, cut:
> 2 strips, each 3¼" x 25½", for sides.
> 2 strips, each 3¼" x 28", for top and bottom.

DIRECTIONS

1. To make a Courthouse Steps block, place the short side of a center rectangle on top of a 1¼"-wide strip; then stitch. You can place more than 1 rectangle on a strip if desired.

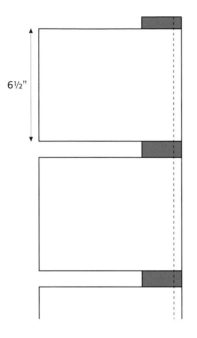

2. Turn the strip and rectangles around, place the opposite short side on top of another 1¼"-wide fabric strip, and stitch.

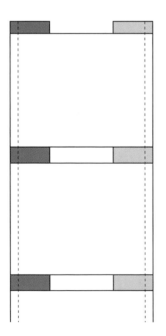

3. Press the seams toward the strips. Trim the ends even with the rectangles.

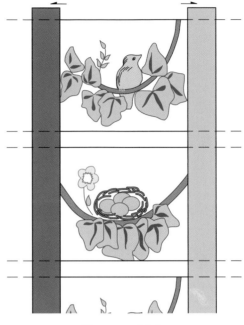

Trim excess fabric.

Woodland Spring by Cleo Nollette, 1998, Seattle, Washington, 28" x 31". Quilted by Clara Stutzman. The center squares of the Courthouse Steps blocks were carefully cut from a printed stripe intended for borders.

4. Repeat steps 1–3 to add strips to the long sides of the rectangles. Then continue adding strips, starting first with the short sides and then going to the long sides. Alternate theme-print strips and green-print strips. Make 6 each of the following blocks.

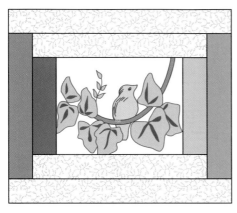

Make 6.

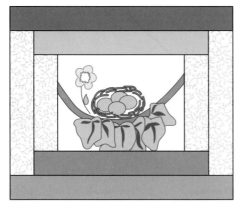

Make 6.

5. Join the blocks in 4 rows of 3 blocks each. Join the rows.

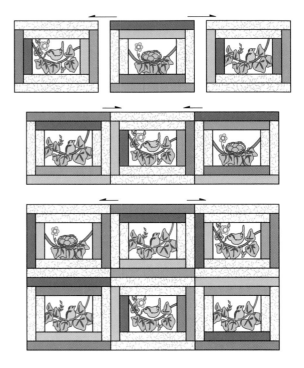

6. Add the 1"-wide inner border strips and the 3¼"-wide outer border strips, referring to "Straight-Cut Borders" on pages 116–117.

7. Layer the quilt top with batting and backing. Tie or quilt as desired. See quilting suggestion below.

8. Bind the edges with bias strips.

Quilt Talk

Double X

Finished Quilt Size: 38" x 51½"
Finished Block Size: 10½"

6 blocks, set 2 across and 3 down with 3"-wide sashing and cornerstones; 4"-wide border

TIME-CRUNCH FEATURES

• Theme Prints (pages 9–10)
• Wide Sashing (page 11)
• Bias Squares (pages 14–15)

MATERIALS

42"-wide fabric

¼ yd. theme print with sayings*
1½ yds. yellow print for background, sashing squares, and border
1 fat quarter each of 9 blue prints
1 yd. yellow-and-blue print for blocks and sashing
1⅝ yds. fabric for backing
½ yd. fabric for 190" of bias binding
42" x 56" piece of batting

* If you can't find a preprinted fabric with sayings, you can write your own sayings on fabric. You can also transfer sayings onto fabric with the help of a computer and photo-transfer methods.

CUTTING

All measurements include ¼"-wide seams.

From the theme print, cut:
6 squares, each 4" x 4", for blocks.

From the yellow print, cut from the lengthwise grain:
2 strips, each 4¼" x 44", for side borders.
2 strips, each 4¼" x 38", for top and bottom borders.

From the remaining yellow print, cut:
9 squares, each 8" x 8", for bias squares.
24 rectangles, each 2¼" x 4", for blocks.
12 squares, each 2⅝" x 2⅝", for pieced sashing squares.

From each of the 9 blue prints, cut:
1 square (9 total), 8" x 8", for bias squares.
3 squares (27 total), each 2⅜" x 2⅜". Cut once diagonally to yield 54 triangles for pieced sashing squares. You will only use 48.

From each of 6 of the blue prints, cut:
1 square (6 total), 4¾" x 4¾". Cut twice diagonally to yield 24 triangles for blocks.

From the yellow-and-blue print, cut:
12 squares, each 4⅜" x 4⅜". Cut once diagonally to yield 24 triangles for blocks.
17 rectangles, each 3½" x 11", for sashing.

DIRECTIONS

1. Pair each 8" yellow square with an 8" blue square, right sides up. Cut and piece 2½"-wide bias strips, following the directions for bias squares on pages 14–15. Cut 72 bias squares, each 2¼" x 2¼".

2. Join the 4" theme-print square, 4 blue 4¾" triangles, and four 4⅜" triangles from the yellow-and-blue print to make the center section. Press the seams away from the theme-print square.

Make 6.

3. Join 12 bias squares, and 4 yellow-print rectangles to the center section to complete 1 Double X block.

Make 6.

4. Join 4 blue 2⅜" triangles and a 2⅝" yellow-print square to make a sashing square. Press the seams away from the yellow-print square. Use 4 different blue prints for each sashing square.

Make 12.

Quilt Talk by Nancy J. Martin, 1999, Woodinville, Washington, 38" x 51½". Quilted by Bena Miller.
Clever sayings printed on the yellow fabric coordinate with the yellow and blue color scheme.

5. Join 2 blocks and 3 sashing strips to make 1 row. Make 3 rows.

Make 3.

6. Join 2 sashing strips and 3 pieced sashing squares to make 1 sashing row. Make 4 sashing rows.

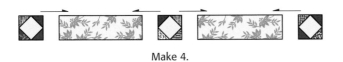

Make 4.

7. Join the rows of blocks and sashing.

8. Add the 4¼"-wide border strips, referring to "Straight-Cut Borders" on pages 116–117.

9. Layer the quilt top with batting and backing. Tie or quilt as desired. See quilting suggestion below.

10. Bind the edges with bias strips.

Quilts in the Attic

Attic Window

Finished Quilt Size: 34" x 34"
Finished Block Size: 8"

9 blocks, set 3 across and 3 down; ¾"-wide inner border; 4¼"-wide outer border

TIME-CRUNCH FEATURES

- Small Quilts (page 9)
- Theme Prints (pages 9–10)

MATERIALS

42"-wide fabric

½ yd. theme print for blocks
⅛ yd. each of 3 light prints for blocks
⅛ yd. each of 3 dark prints for blocks
¼ yd. dark print for inner border
⅜ yd. light print for outer border
⅜ yd. dark print for outer border
1⅛ yds. fabric for backing
⅜ yd. fabric for 146" of bias binding
38" x 38" piece of batting

CUTTING

All measurements include ¼"-wide seams.

From the theme print, cut:
9 squares, each 6½" x 6½", for blocks.

From each of the light prints for blocks, cut:
3 rectangles (9 total), each 2½" x 8¾", for blocks.

From each of the dark prints for blocks, cut:
3 rectangles (9 total), each 2½" x 8¾", for blocks.

From the dark print for inner border, cut:
2 strips, each 1¼" x 24½", for sides.
2 strips, each 1¼" x 26", for top and bottom.

From the light print for outer border, cut:
1 strip, 4½" x 31", for top.
1 strip, 4½" x 36", for left side.

From the dark print for outer border, cut:
1 strip, 4½" x 31", for right side.
1 strip, 4½" x 36", for bottom.

DIRECTIONS

1. Join a light rectangle to the left side of a 6½" square and a dark rectangle to the bottom of the square. End stitching ¼" from the lower left corner of the square.

2. Miter the corner of the light and dark rectangles, referring to steps 6–8 in "Borders with Mitered Corners" on page 118.

Make 9.

3. Join the blocks in 3 rows of 3 blocks each. Join the rows.
4. Add the 1¼"-wide inner border strips, referring to "Straight-Cut Borders" on pages 116–117.
5. Join the outer border strips to the quilt top in the order shown. End the stitching ¼" from the upper right and lower left corners of the quilt top.

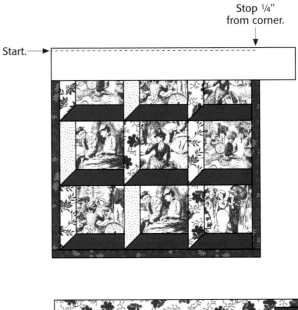

Quilts in the Attic by Cleo Nollette, 1998, Seattle, Washington, 34" x 34". Quilted by Sarah Troyer. Cut from a toile, the center square of each Attic Window block highlights a character or scene related to quilting.

6. Miter the upper right and lower left corners, referring to steps 6–8 of "Borders with Mitered Borders" on page 118.

7. Layer the quilt top with batting and backing. Tie or quilt as desired. See quilting suggestion below.

8. Bind the edges with bias strips.

Sew and Sew

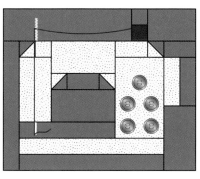

Sew and Sew

Finished Quilt Size: 18½" x 36½"
Finished Block Size: 12" x 10"

3 blocks, set vertically; 1½"-wide inner border; 1½"-wide outer border

TIME-CRUNCH FEATURES

- Small Quilts (page 9)
- Easiest Pieced Border in the World (pages 17–18)

MATERIALS

42"-wide fabric

1 fat quarter each of 3 light prints for sewing machine
1 fat quarter each of 3 medium prints for background
8 strips, each 2" x 20", of assorted dark prints for pieced outer borders
Scrap of red print for spool of thread
¼ yd. beige print for inner border
¾ yd. fabric for backing
¼ yd. fabric for 120" of bias binding
5 buttons, ¾"–1" diameter
23" x 41" piece of batting

CUTTING

All measurements include ¼"-wide seams.

From beige print, cut:
2 strips, each 2" x 30½", for inner side borders.
2 strips, each 2" x 15½", for inner top and bottom borders.

DIRECTIONS

1. Cut and piece 3 blocks, using pieces 1–18. Cutting directions are for 1 block.

Piece No.	Fabric	No. of Pieces	Dimensions
1	Light	2	2½" x 4½"
2	Light	2	1⅞" x 1⅞" ◩
3	Light	1	1½" x 1½"
4	Light	1	1½" x 2½"
5	Light	1	3½" x 5½"
6	Light	1	1½" x 3½"
7	Light	1	1½" x 9½"
8	Red	1	1½" x 1½"
9	Medium	1	2½" x 8½"
10	Medium	1	1½" x 1½"
11	Medium	1	2½" x 3½"
12	Medium	2	1½" x 2½"
13	Medium	2	1⅞" x 1⅞" ◩
14	Medium	2	2½" x 4½"
15	Medium	1	1½" x 3½"
16	Medium	1	1½" x 8½"
17	Medium	1	1½" x 7½"
18	Medium	1	1½" x 9½"

◩ = cut squares once diagonally

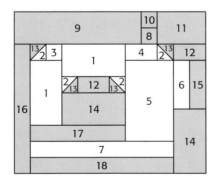

2. Zigzag stitch a thread guide and a needle with white thread. Use a heavyweight thread, such as Mettler Cordonnet, to stitch a line of thread from the spool, through the thread guide, and down to the needle.

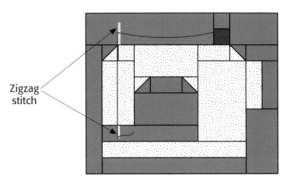

Zigzag stitch

3. Join the blocks in one vertical row.
4. Add the 2"-wide border strips, referring to "Straight-Cut Borders" on pages 116–117.
5. Join the 2" x 20" dark strips to make a strip unit. Cut 9 segments, each 2" wide, from the strip unit.

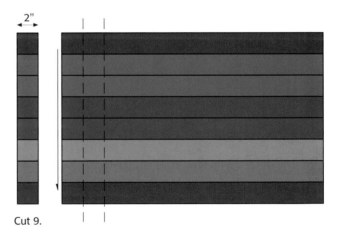

2"

Cut 9.

6. Remove 2 squares from 1 of the 9 segments. Add the squares to an 8-square segment for a total of 10 squares. Repeat, removing 2 more squares and attaching them to another 8-square segment. Stitch the two 10-square segments to the top and bottom edges of the quilt top.

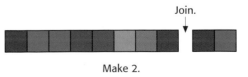

Join.

Make 2.

Sew and Sew by Nancy J. Martin, 1999, Woodinville, Washington, 18½" x 36½". Quilted by Mary Hershberger. Large buttons represent the dials on my favorite sewing machine.

7. Join 3 of the 8-square segments end to end, for a total of 24 squares, to make 1 of the side borders; repeat. Add the 2 side borders to opposite sides of the quilt.

8. Layer the quilt top with batting and backing. Tie or quilt as desired. See quilting suggestion below.

9. Bind the edges with bias strips.

10. Add buttons for sewing machine knobs.

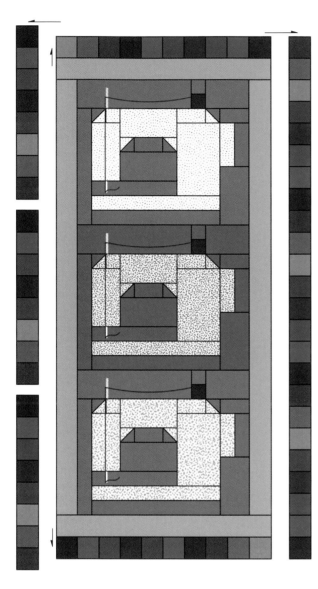

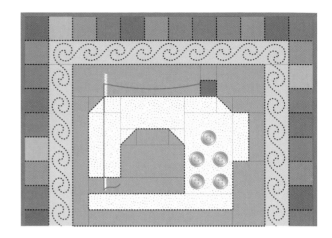

Three Little Pumpkins

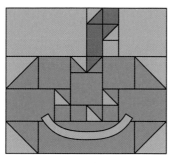

Pumpkin

Finished Quilt Size: 44" x 23"
Finished Block Size: 10" x 9"

3 blocks, set horizontally; 4"-wide border

TIME-CRUNCH FEATURE

- Bias-Strip Appliqué (pages 13–14)

MATERIALS

42"-wide fabric

1 fat quarter of light orange print for blocks
1 fat eighth each of 3 orange prints for blocks
1/8 yd. brown print for fence
1/8 yd. green print for grass and blocks
1/4 yd. medium print for border
1/4 yd. dark print for border
1 3/8 yd. fabric for backing
3/8 yd. fabric for 146" of bias binding
49" x 28" piece of batting

CUTTING

All measurements include 1/4"-wide seams.

From the light orange print, cut:
   4 strips, each 2" x 6 1/2", for fence posts.

From the brown print, cut:
   1 strip, 2" x 42", for fence.
   4 strips, each 2" x 11", for fence posts.

From the green print, cut:
   1 strip, 2" x 42", for grass.

From the medium print, cut:
   1 strip, 4 1/4" x 36 1/2", for top border.
   2 strips, 4 1/4" x 16", for side borders.

From the dark print, cut:
   1 strip, 4 1/4" x 36 1/2", for bottom border.
   2 strips, 4 1/4" x 16", for side borders.

DIRECTIONS

1. Cut and piece 3 blocks, using pieces 1–14. Appliqué piece 15 (see page 13). Cutting directions are for 1 block.

Piece No.	Fabric	No. of Pieces	Dimensions
1	Light orange	1	3½" x 5½"
2	Light orange	3	1⅞" x 1⅞" ◩
3	Light orange	1	1½" x 1½"
4	Light orange	1	3½" x 3½"
5	Light orange	2	2⅞" x 2⅞" ◩
6	Green	2	1⅞" x 1⅞" ◩
7	Green	1	1½" x 1½"
8	Green	1	1½" x 2½"
9	Orange	2	2⅞" x 2⅞" ◩
10	Orange	3	2½" x 2½"
11	Orange	3	1⅞" x 1⅞" ◩
12	Orange	2	2½" x 3½"
13	Orange	3	1½" x 1½"
14	Orange	1	2½" x 6½"
15	Light orange	1	1¼" x 6" bias strip for appliqué

◩ = cut squares once diagonally

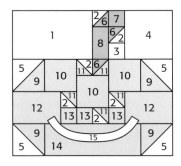

2. Join the 2" x 42" brown strips and green strips to make a strip set. Crosscut the strip set into 3 segments, each 10½" wide, for the fence units.

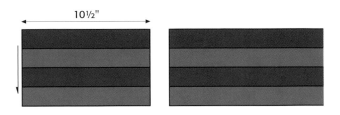

10½"

3. Join the 2" x 6½" light orange strips and 2" x 11" brown strips to make fence posts.

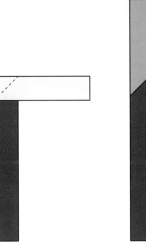

Make 2.

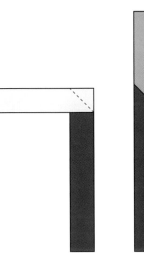

Make 2.

Three Little Pumpkins by Nancy J. Martin, 1999, Woodinville, Washington, 44" x 23". Quilted by Clara Troyer. This festive banner is the perfect Halloween accent.

4. Join the Pumpkin blocks, fence units, and fence posts.

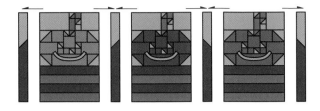

5. Join the 4¼" x 36½" medium print to the top of the quilt top and the 4¼" x 36½" dark print to the bottom.

6. Join the 4¼" x 16" medium print and dark print strips to make left and right borders.

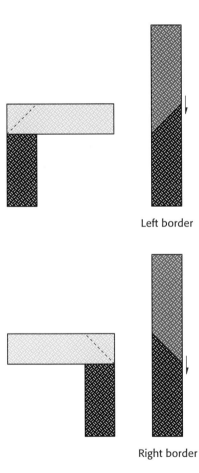

Left border

Right border

7. Join the borders to opposite sides, matching the 45° angle on the border strips with the 45° angle on the fence posts. Trim the excess border strips on the top and bottom edges.

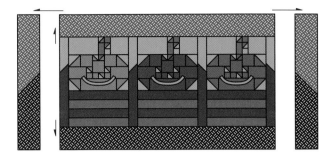

8. Layer the quilt top with batting and backing. Tie or quilt as desired. See quilting suggestion below.

9. Bind the edges with bias strips.

Tea Party

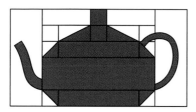

Teapot

Teacup Creamer Sugar Bowl

Finished Quilt Size: 19½" x 24¾"
Finished Block Sizes:

 Sugar Bowl – 4" x 3½"
 Creamer – 6" x 3½"
 Teapot – 11" x 6"
 Teacup – 5" x 3½"

5 blocks, set in 3 rows with 1"-wide sashing; 1"-wide inner border; 3¼"-wide outer border

TIME-CRUNCH FEATURE

• Bias-Strip Appliqué (pages 13–14)

MATERIALS

42"-wide fabric

¼ yd. light pink print for background
¼ yd. red print #1 for blocks
¼ yd. red print #2 for blocks and outer border
¼ yd. red print #3 for sashing and inner border
⅝ yd. fabric for backing
¼ yd. fabric for 100" of bias binding
24" x 29" piece of batting

CUTTING

All measurements include ¼"-wide seams. Use Template A on page 115.

From the light pink print, cut:
 2 strips, each 1" x 4", for background.
 1 strip, 1½" x 4", for background.
 1 strip, 1" x 11½", for background.
 1 strip, 1¼" x 11½", for background.

From red print #2, cut:
 2 strips, each 3½" x 18¾", for outer side borders.
 2 strips, each 3½" x 19½", for outer top and bottom borders.

From red print #3, cut:
 2 strips, each 1½" x 11½", for horizontal sashing.
 2 strips, each 1½" x 16¾", for inner side borders.
 2 strips, each 1½" x 13½", for inner top and bottom borders.

DIRECTIONS

1. Make the following blocks.

Sugar Bowl

Cut and piece 1 block using pieces 1–5.

Piece No.	Fabric	No. of Pieces	Dimensions
1	Light pink	2	1" x 2¼"
2 & 2r	Light pink	2 each	Template A and A reversed
3	Red #1	1	1" x 1"
4 & 4r	Red #1	2 each	Template A and A reversed
5	Red #1	1	2½" x 2½"

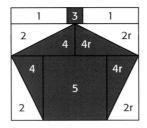

Creamer

Cut and piece 1 block, using pieces 1–9. Appliqué piece 10 (see page 13).

Piece No.	Fabric	No. of Pieces	Dimensions
1	Light pink	1	1" x 6½"
2	Light pink	1	1⅞" x 1⅞" ◹
3	Light pink	1	1½" x 2½"
4 & 4r	Light pink	1 each	Template A and A reversed
5	Light pink	1	1½" x 3½"
6	Red #1	1	1⅞" x 1⅞" ◹
7 & 7r	Red #1	1 each	Template A and A reversed
8	Red #1	1	1½" x 4½"
9	Red #1	1	2½" x 2½"
10	Red #1	1	1" x 5" bias strip for appliqué

◹ = cut squares once diagonally

Tea Party by Nancy J. Martin, 1999, Woodinville, Washington, 19½" x 24¾". Quilted by Clara Stutzman. A charming tea service and cups suggest a party.

Teapot

Cut and piece 1 block, using pieces 1–10. Appliqué pieces 11 and 12 (see page 13).

Piece No.	Fabric	No. of Pieces	Dimensions
1	Light pink	2	2½" x 6½"
2	Light pink	2	1½" x 3½"
3	Light pink	2	1½" x 1½"
4 & 4r	Light pink	1 each	Template A and A reversed
5	Light pink	2	1⅞" x 1⅞" ◹
6	Red #1	2	1½" x 1½"
7 & 7r	Red #1	1 each	Template A and A reversed
8	Red #1	2	1⅞" x 1⅞" ◹
9	Red #1	2	1½" x 5½"
10	Red #1	1	2½" x 7½"
11	Red #1	1	1½" x 5" bias strip for appliqué
12	Red #1	1	1" x 8" bias strip for appliqué

◹ = cut squares once diagonally

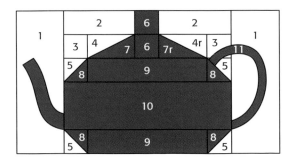

Teacup

Cut and piece 2 blocks, using pieces 1–8. Appliqué piece 9 (see page 13). Cutting directions are for 1 block.

Piece No.	Fabric	No. of Pieces	Dimensions
1 & 1r	Light pink	1 each	Template A and A reversed
2	Light pink	1	1⅜" x 1⅜" ◹
3	Light pink	1	1½" x 4"
4	Red #2	1	1½" x 4½"
5 & 5r	Red #2	1 each	Template A and A reversed
6	Red #2	1	2½" x 2½"
7	Red #2	1	1" x 3½"
8	Red #2	1	1⅜" x 1⅜" ◹
9	Red #2	1	1" x 5" bias strip for appliqué

◹ = cut squares once diagonally

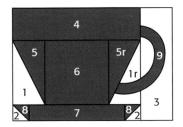

2. Join the blocks, additional background pieces, and sashing strips.

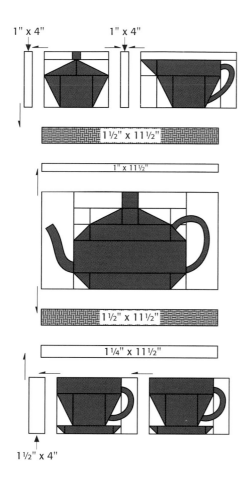

3. Add the 1½"-wide inner border strips, and 3½"-wide outer border strips, referring to "Straight-Cut Borders" on pages 116–117.
4. Layer the quilt top with batting and backing. Tie or quilt as desired. See quilting suggestion below.
5. Bind the edges with bias strips.

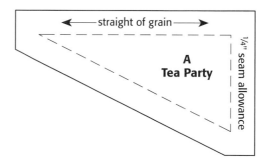

Finishing

BORDERS

Time is of the essence when making a time-crunch quilt, so it's best to try to avoid pieced borders unless you are using the "easiest pieced border in the world" (pages 17–18). Straight-cut borders are the simplest to add, but it's important to take a few preliminary steps to make sure the border lies flat.

To begin, straighten the edge of your quilt top before adding borders. There should be little or no trimming needed for a straight-set quilt. Next, to find the correct measurement for border strips, always measure through the center of the quilt, not at the outside edges. This ensures that the borders are of equal length on opposite sides of the quilt and brings the outer edges in line with the center dimension if discrepancies exist. Otherwise, your quilt might not be square due to minor piecing variations and/or stretching that occurred while you worked with the pieces. If there is a large difference between the two sides, it is better to go back and correct the source of the problem rather than try to make the border fit and end up with a distorted quilt.

Borders are commonly cut along the crosswise grain and seamed where extra length is needed. The seam will be less noticeable and stronger if it is pieced on an angle. You may need additional fabric to do so.

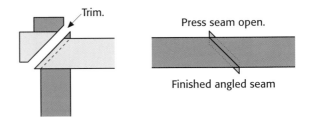

Borders cut from the lengthwise grain of fabric require extra yardage, but seaming to achieve the required length is then unnecessary.

Straight-Cut Borders

The simplest border to add is a straight-cut border. This method has been used on most of the quilts with borders in this book. You will save fabric if you attach the border to the longer sides first, then stitch the border to the remaining two sides.

1. Measure the length of the quilt at the center. Cut 2 border strips to this measurement, piecing as necessary.

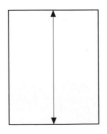

Measure center of
quilt, top to bottom.

2. Mark the centers of the border strips and the quilt top. Pin the borders to the sides of the quilt, matching centers and ends and easing or slightly stretching the quilt to fit the border strip as necessary.

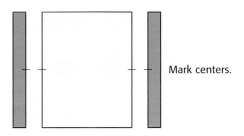

Mark centers.

3. Sew the side borders in place and press the seams toward the borders.

4. Measure the center width of the quilt, including the side borders, to determine the length of the top and bottom borders. Cut 2 border strips to this measurement, piecing strips as necessary. Mark the centers of the border strips and the quilt top. Pin borders to the top and bottom of the quilt top, easing or slightly stretching the quilt to fit as necessary.

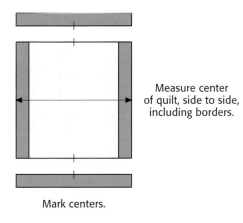

Measure center of quilt, side to side, including borders.

Mark centers.

5. Sew the top and bottom borders in place and press the seams toward the borders.

Borders with Corner Squares

Applying borders with corner squares is an economical use of fabric since you can use shorter border strips. Corner squares may be plain

squares of matching or contrasting fabric, or they may be pieced squares.

1. Measure the width and length of the quilt top through the center. Cut border strips to those measurements, piecing as necessary.

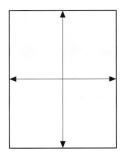

2. Mark the center of the quilt edges and the border strips. Pin the side border strips to opposite sides of the quilt top, matching centers and ends and easing as necessary; stitch. Press the seams toward the border.

3. Cut corner squares the required size, which is the cut width of the border strips. Sew one corner square to each end of the remaining two border strips; press the seams toward the border strips. Pin the border strips to the top and bottom edges of the quilt top. Match centers, seams, and ends, easing as necessary; stitch. Press the seams toward the border.

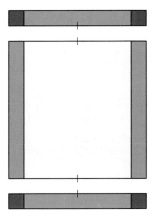

Borders with Mitered Corners

Mitered borders have a diagonal seam where the borders meet in the corners. If your quilt has multiple borders, sew the individual strips together and treat the resulting unit as a single border strip.

1. First estimate the finished outside dimensions of your quilt, including borders. Border strips should be cut to this length plus at least ½" for seam allowances. Add 3"–4" to be safer and to give you some leeway.
2. Mark the center of the quilt edges and the border strips.
3. Measure the length and width of the quilt top across the center. Note the measurements.
4. Place a pin at each end of the side border strips to mark the length of the quilt top. Repeat with the top and bottom borders.

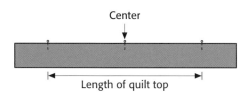

Center

Length of quilt top

5. Pin the borders to the quilt top, matching the centers. Line up the pins at either end of the border strip with the quilt edges. Stitch, beginning and ending the stitching ¼" from the raw edges of the quilt top. Repeat with the remaining borders.

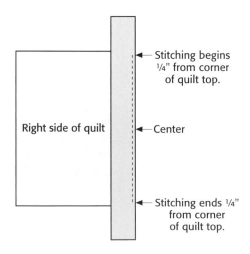

Stitching begins ¼" from corner of quilt top.

Right side of quilt

Center

Stitching ends ¼" from corner of quilt top.

6. Lay the first corner to be mitered on the ironing board. Fold under 1 border strip at a 45° angle to the other strip. Press and pin.

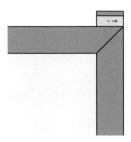

7. Fold the quilt with right sides together, lining up the edges of the border. If necessary, use a ruler and pencil to draw a line on the crease to make the line more visible. Stitch on the pressed crease, sewing from the corner to the outside edges.

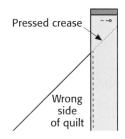

Pressed crease

Wrong side of quilt

8. Press the seam open and trim away excess border strips, leaving a ¼"-wide seam allowance.
9. Repeat with remaining corners.

MARKING THE QUILT

Mark a design to be quilted on the quilt top unless you are doing one of the following: quilting in the ditch; outlining the design ¼" from all seams; or stitching a grid of straight lines, using ¼"-wide masking tape as a guide.

To stitch in the ditch, place the stitches in the valley created next to a seam. Stitch on the side that does not have the seam allowance under it.

Quilting in the ditch

To outline a design, stitch ¼" from the seam inside each shape.

Outline quilting

To mark a grid or pattern of lines, use ¼"-wide masking tape in 15" to 18" lengths. Place strips of tape on a small area and quilt next to the edge of the tape. Remove the tape when stitching is complete. You can reuse the tape to mark another area.

Masking tape

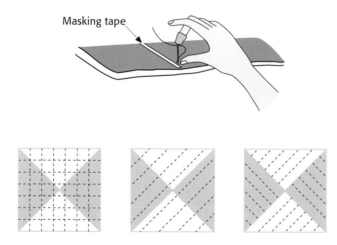

To mark complex designs, use a stencil. Quilting stencils made from durable plastic are available in quilt shops. Use stencils to mark repeated designs. There is a groove cut in the plastic, wide enough to allow the use of a marking device. Just place the marker inside the

groove to quickly transfer the design to the fabric. Good removable marking pencils include Berol silver pencils, EZ Washout marking pencils, mechanical pencils, and sharp regular pencils. Just be sure to draw lines lightly. Test any marking device on a scrap of fabric for removability.

Use a light table to trace designs that are more intricate. To make your own light table, separate your dining room table as if adding an extra leaf. Then place a piece of glass, plastic, or Plexiglas over the opening. Have the glass (or glass substitute) cut to fit your table at a glass shop, if desired, and frame or tape the edges to avoid cut fingers. For an additional fee, you can have the glass edges finished to eliminate the sharp edges. For safety's sake, I use a removable glass storm door that has a frame around the edge of the glass.

Once the glass is in place, position a table lamp on the floor beneath the table to create an instant light table. If your table does not separate, two card tables or end tables of the same height can be pushed together to create support for the glass.

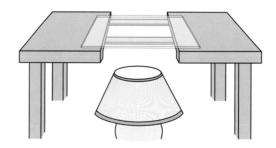

BACKING

For most quilts larger than crib size, you will need to piece the backing from two or more strips of fabric if you use 42"-wide fabric. Seams can run horizontally (crosswise join) or vertically (lengthwise join) in a pieced backing, as long as the fabric isn't a directional print. Avoid the temptation to use a bed sheet for a backing, as it is difficult to quilt through. Cut backing 3" to 4" larger than the quilt top all around. Be sure to trim away the selvages where pieces are joined.

If you plan to hang your quilt, you will need to put a sleeve or rod pocket on the back of the quilt (see page 126). Purchase extra backing fabric so that the sleeve and the backing match. Once you know the finished size of your quilt, refer to the following illustrations to plan the backing layout and to determine how much fabric you'll need.

Sometimes the backing fabric is just a little too narrow for a quilt. Pieced backs are fun to make, and they can be the answer to this annoying problem.

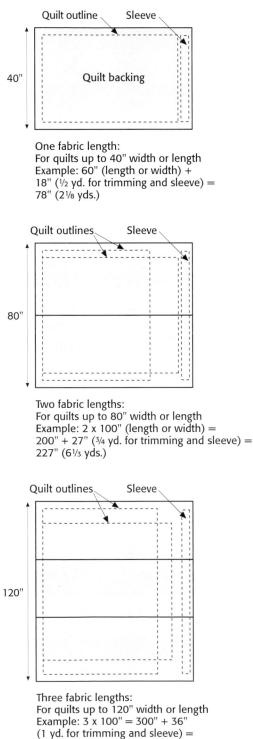

One fabric length:
For quilts up to 40" width or length
Example: 60" (length or width) +
18" (½ yd. for trimming and sleeve) =
78" (2⅛ yds.)

Two fabric lengths:
For quilts up to 80" width or length
Example: 2 x 100" (length or width) =
200" + 27" (¾ yd. for trimming and sleeve) =
227" (6⅓ yds.)

Three fabric lengths:
For quilts up to 120" width or length
Example: 3 x 100" = 300" + 36"
(1 yd. for trimming and sleeve) =
336" (9⅓ yds.)

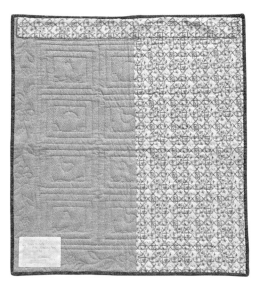

You can also use scraps of fabric from your sewing stash, piecing them together to form a backing large enough for your quilt top. This is most effective when you use some of the fabrics that were used on the front of the quilt.

BATTING

There are many types of batting to choose from. Select a high-loft batting for a bed quilt that you want to look puffy. Lightweight battings are fine for baby quilts or wall hangings. A lightweight batting is easier to quilt through and shows the quilting design well. It also resembles antique quilts, giving an old-fashioned look.

Polyester batting works well, doesn't shift after washing, and is easy to quilt through. It comes in lightweight and regular lofts as well as in a fat batting for comforters.

Cotton batting is a good choice if you are quilting an old quilt top. Most cotton batting must be quilted with stitches no more than 2" apart. There are, however, several new cotton battings available today that may be quilted up to 8" apart. Be sure to read the manufacturer's directions to determine the type of batting you have.

Dark batting works well behind a dark quilt top. If there is any bearding (batting fibers creeping through the top), it will not be as noticeable.

LAYERING AND BASTING

Open a package of batting and smooth it out flat. Allow the batting to rest in this position for at least twenty-four hours. Press the backing so that all seams are flat and the fold lines have been removed.

A large dining-room table, Ping-Pong table, or two large folding tables pushed together make an ideal work surface on which to prepare your quilt. Use a table pad to protect your dining-room table. The floor is not a good choice for layering your quilt. It requires too much bending, and the layers can easily shift or be disturbed.

Place the backing on the table with the wrong side of the fabric facing up. If the table is large enough, you may want to tape the backing down with masking tape. Spread your batting over the backing, centering it, and smooth out any remaining folds.

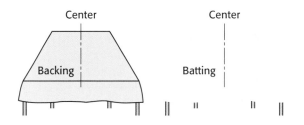

Center the freshly pressed and marked quilt top on these two layers. Check all four sides to make sure there is adequate batting and backing. Stretch the backing to make sure it is still smooth.

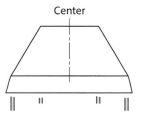

The basting method you use depends on whether you will quilt by hand or by machine. Thread basting is generally used for hand quilting, while safety-pin basting is used for machine quilting.

Thread Basting

Starting in the middle of the quilt top, baste the three layers together with straight pins while gently smoothing out the fullness to the sides and corners. Take care not to distort the straight lines of the quilt design and the borders.

After pinning, baste the layers together with a needle and light-colored thread. (Dark-colored thread may bleed onto the quilt.) Start in the middle and make a line of long stitches to each corner to form a large **X**.

Continue basting in a grid of parallel lines 6" to 8" apart. Finish with a row of basting around the outside edges. Quilts that are to be quilted with a hoop or on your lap will be handled more than those quilted on a frame; therefore, they require more basting. After basting, remove the pins. Now you are ready to quilt.

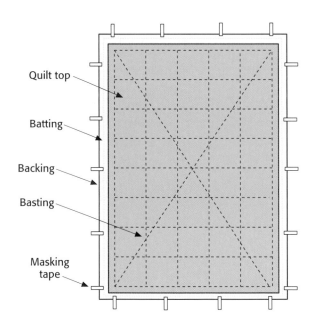

Quilt top
Batting
Backing
Basting
Masking tape

Pin Basting

A quick way to baste a quilt top is with size 2 safety pins. They are large enough to catch all three layers but not so large that they snag fine fabric. Begin pinning in the center and work out toward the edges. Place pins 4" to 5" apart.

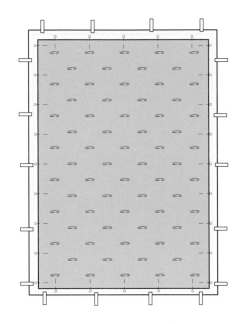

Baste around the outside edge with straight pins to hold everything in place.

QUILTING

Hand Quilting

To quilt by hand, you need quilting thread, quilting needles, small scissors, a thimble, and perhaps a balloon or large rubber band to help grasp the needle if it gets stuck. Quilt on a frame, a large hoop, or on your lap or a table. Use a single strand of quilting thread no longer than 18". Make a small, single knot at the end of the thread. The quilting stitch is a small running stitch that goes through all three layers of the quilt. Take two, three, even four stitches at a time if you can keep them even. When crossing seams, you might find it necessary to "hunt and peck" one stitch at a time.

To begin, insert the needle in the top layer about 1" from the point you want to start stitching. Pull the needle out at the starting point and gently tug at the knot until it pops through the fabric and is buried in the batting. Make a back-stitch and begin quilting. Stitches should be tiny (eight to ten per inch is good), even, and straight; tiny will come with practice.

When you come almost to the end of the thread, make a single knot ¼" from the fabric. Take a backstitch to bury the knot in the bat-ting. Run the thread off through the batting and out the quilt top; then snip it off. The first and last stitches will look different from the running stitches in between. To make them less noticeable, start and stop where quilting lines cross each other or at seam joints.

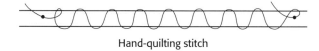

Hand-quilting stitch

Machine Quilting

A walking foot or even-feed foot is essential for straight-line and grid quilting and for large, simple curves. It helps feed the quilt layers through the machine without shifting or puck-ering. Read the machine instruction manual for special tension settings to sew through extra fabric thicknesses.

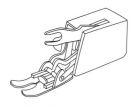

Walking foot attachment

If your project has intricately curved designs, use a darning foot and lower the feed dogs for free-motion quilting. Free-motion quilting allows the fabric to move freely under the foot of the sewing machine. Because the feed dogs are lowered, the stitch length is determined by the speed at which you run the machine and feed the fabric under the foot. Practice on a layer of

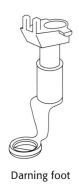

Darning foot

fabric scraps until you get the feel of controlling the motion of the fabric with your hands. Run the machine fairly fast, since this makes it easier to sew smoother lines of quilt-ing. Do not turn the fabric under the needle. Instead, guide the fabric as if it were under a stationary pencil (the needle).

Stitch some free-form scribbles, zigzags, and curves. Try a heart or a star. Free-motion quilt-ing may feel awkward at first, but with a little determination and practice, you can imitate beautiful hand-quilting designs quickly and complete a project in just a few hours.

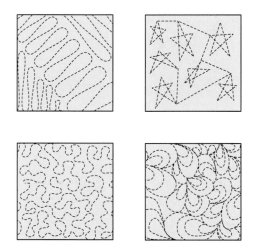

When machine quilting, keep the spacing between quilting lines consistent over the entire project. Avoid using complex, little designs and leaving large spaces unquilted. With most battings, a 2" to 3" square is the largest area that can be left unquilted. Also, do not try to machine quilt an entire quilt in one sitting, even if it's a small quilt. Break the work into short periods, and stretch and relax your muscles regularly.

Finally, when all the quilting has been completed, remove the safety pins. However, sometimes it is necessary to remove safety pins as you work.

BINDING

My favorite quilt binding is a double-fold French binding made from bias strips. It rolls over the edges of the quilt nicely, and the two layers of fabric resist wear. If you use 2¼"-wide strips, the finished width of this binding will be ⅜".

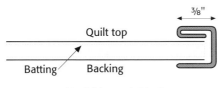

Double-fold French binding

The quilt directions tell you how much fabric to purchase for binding. If, however, you enlarge your quilt, you'll need to measure the distance around your quilt and add about 10" for turning the corners and for overlapping the ends of the binding strips. Use this handy chart to compute how much binding you'll need:

Length of Binding	Fabric Needed
115"	¼ yd.*
180"	⅜ yd.*
255"	½ yd.
320"	⅝ yd.
400"	¾ yd.
465"	⅞ yd.

* It is a good idea to purchase ½ yard of fabric instead of ¼ or ⅜ yard so the bias strips will be longer and the binding won't have as many seams.

After quilting, trim excess batting and backing even with the edge of the quilt top. A rotary cutter and long ruler will ensure accurate straight edges. If the basting is no longer in place, baste all three layers together at the outside edges. If you are going to attach a sleeve to the back of your quilt for hanging, turn to page 126 and attach it now, before you bind the edges.

To cut bias strips, follow these steps:

1. Align the 45° marking of the Bias Square along the selvage and place the ruler's edge against it. Make the first cut.

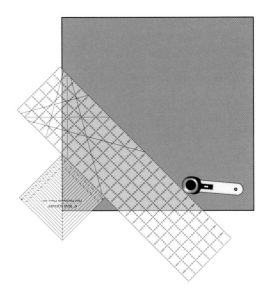

2. Measure the width of the strip, 2¼", from the cut edge of the fabric. Cut along the edge of the ruler.

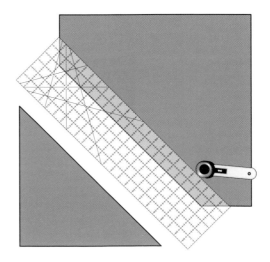

When cutting bias strips, a 24"-long ruler may be too short for some of the cuts. After making several cuts, carefully fold the fabric over itself so that the bias edges are even. Continue to cut bias strips.

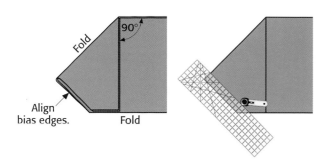

Follow these steps to bind the edges:

1. Stitch bias strips together, offsetting them as shown. Press the seams open.

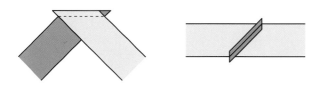

2. Fold the strip in half lengthwise, wrong sides together, and press.

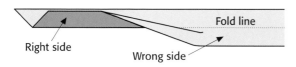

3. Unfold the binding at 1 end and turn under ¼" at a 45° angle as shown.

4. Starting on 1 side of the quilt, stitch the binding to the quilt. Use a ¼"-wide seam allowance. Begin stitching 1" to 2" from the start of the binding. Stop stitching ¼" from the corner and backstitch.

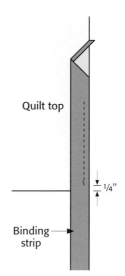

5. Turn the quilt to prepare for sewing along the next edge. Fold the binding away from the quilt, then fold again to place the binding along the second edge of the quilt. This fold creates an angled pleat at the corner.

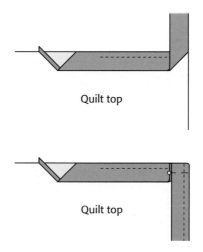

6. Stitch from the fold of the binding along the second edge of the quilt top, stopping ¼" from the corner as you did for the first corner; backstitch. Repeat the stitching and mitering process on the remaining edges and corners of the quilt.

7. When you reach the beginning of the binding, cut the end 1" longer than needed and tuck the end inside the beginning. Stitch the rest of the binding.

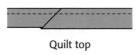

Quilt top

8. Turn the binding to the back side, over the raw edges of the quilt. Blindstitch in place, with the folded edge covering the row of machine stitching. At each corner, fold the binding to form a miter on the back of the quilt.

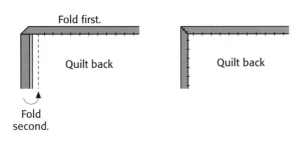

QUILT SLEEVES

If you plan to hang your quilt, attach a sleeve or rod pocket to the back before attaching the binding. From the leftover backing fabric, cut an 8"-wide strip of fabric equal to the width of your quilt. You may need to piece two or three strips together for larger quilts. On each end, fold over ½" and then fold ½" again. Press and stitch by machine.

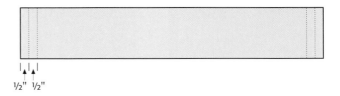

½" ½"

Fold the strip in half lengthwise, wrong sides together; baste the raw edges to the top edge of the back of your quilt. These will be secured when you sew on the binding. Your quilt should be about 1" wider than the sleeve on both sides. Make a little pleat in the sleeve to accommodate the thickness of the rod, then slipstitch the ends and bottom edge of the sleeve to the backing fabric. This keeps the rod from being inserted next to the quilt backing.

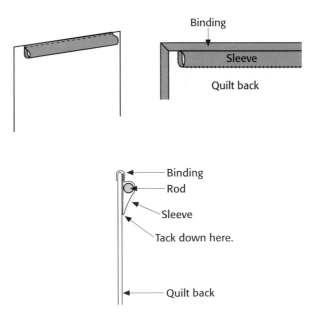

QUILT LABELS

It's a good idea to label a quilt with its name, the name and address of the maker, and the date it was made. Include the name of the quilter(s) if the quilt was quilted by a group or someone other than the maker. On an antique quilt, record all the information you know about the quilt, including where you purchased it. If the quilt is being presented to someone as a gift, also include that information.

To make a label, use a permanent-ink pen to print or legibly write all this information on a piece of muslin. Press freezer paper to the back of the muslin to stabilize it while you write. Press raw edges to the wrong side of the label.

Remove the freezer paper and stitch the label securely to the lower corner of the quilt. You can also do labels in cross-stitch or embroidery.

About the Author

Nancy J. Martin, talented author, teacher, and quiltmaker, has written more than thirty books on quiltmaking. Nancy is an innovator in the quilting industry and introduced the Bias Square cutting ruler to quilters everywhere. Along with more than twenty years of teaching experience and numerous classic quilting titles to her credit, Nancy is the founder and president of Martingale & Company, the publisher of America's Best-Loved Quilt Books®. Nancy and her husband, Dan, enjoy living in the Pacific Northwest.

Books from
Martingale & Company